Completely Connected

Completely Connected

Uniting Our Empathy and Insight
for Extraordinary Results

RITA MARIE JOHNSON

RASUR
MEDIA
IRVING, TEXAS

What Others Are Saying About This Book

"*Completely Connected* is brilliant, authentic and potent. Rita Marie Johnson puts leading edge theory into groundbreaking practice and offers us a medicine that is both soulful and acutely relevant."
— James O'Dea, author of *The Conscious Activist, Cultivating Peace* and other works, Colorado

"In *Completely Connected,* Johnson draws from scientific evidence and her extensive personal experience to produce a work that is eminently readable and convincing. This is transformative learning at its best and makes a vital contribution to peace theory, education and action. People of all ages and walks of life—from school children to octogenarians, from educators to business, nonprofit, government and social-service leaders—are offered a skill that transcends polarizing win-lose approaches to conflict. Readers learn how to combine empathy and insight to achieve astonishing results—results that include improved grades and performance and also heal, empower, and humanize."
— Dr. Patricia Mische, co-founder of Global Education Associates and author, Washington, D.C.

"In business, relationship conflicts are the primary driver of inefficiency—not to mention stress. This book shows how to stop the conflicts and, instead, tap collective creativity and improve buy-in for greater results."
— Anita Campion, President and CEO, Connexus, a global consulting firm, Washington, D.C.

"Rita Marie Johnson has helped thousands of Costa Rican children and teachers prevent school violence through her connection method. I hope this book will help spread the experience to schools and other organizations throughout the world."
— Carlos Francisco Echeverría, former Minister of Culture, Costa Rica

"If more people followed this path, we would have a more peaceful, just and humane world. *Completely Connected* should be required reading for all our schoolchildren, who will soon be the future leaders in this country."
— Dr. Rick Halperin, Director, Embrey Human Rights Program, Southern Methodist University, Texas

"Organizations need people who know and are comfortable with themselves and are able to understand and relate to others. This book delivers the tools for people to do exactly that."
— Dr. Carol Gallagher, Managing Partner, Alliance for Excellence, California

"The book catapults readers into a new level of personal empowerment through a marriage between who they were before experiencing the Connection Practice and who they will inevitably become after learning it."
— Dr. Doreatha Fields, Founder of the Diamond School, Florida

"This amazingly effective technique dramatically transforms relationships—not only those between people, but just as importantly the relationship with ourselves. It is a quantum leap in turning our impossible conflicts into meaningful, fulfilling connections."
— David McArthur, J.D, coauthor, *The Intelligent Heart*, California

"Rita Marie Johnson is a master teacher and peacebuilder who brilliantly blends modern science and practical skills to empower people to communicate effectively from their hearts, even in difficult situations. Rita Marie's work is appropriate for people of all ages and cultures; and, it is helping to create a global culture of peace."
— Philip M. Hellmich, Director of Peace, The Shift Network, author of *God and Conflict: A Search for Peace in a Time of Crisis*, California

"When parents, educators, heads of state and federal government, and those that aspire to become world leaders read this book and practice its tools, war will be a thing of the past and hunger won't have a home."
— Lee and Diane Brandenburg, Brandenburg Family Foundation, California

"I've always had a vision of peace being possible in this world, but have felt helpless in finding a tangible way to move toward this goal. I now see a way this can happen by supporting one person at a time to learn this practice. This book has inspired me to get more involved in growing this within my community."
— Michael Deese, CEO, Visionary Products Inc., Texas

"This simple process provides skills and a roadmap to help me shift out of life-alienating programming into compassion for myself and others. Life is so much richer."
— J. Lynn McDonald, professional mediator, Texas

"Ever since the first time I experienced Rita Marie's innovative Connection Practice, it was clear that it has incredible power to transform individuals, families and organizations. In fact, it has brought much peace to my own life and the lives of those I've coached. Now everyone can benefit from her work and its success through this great new book. Bravo, Rita Marie!"
— Susan M. Beck, Founder/President, Global Future Unlimited, Missouri

"Learning how to override the part of my brain that is irrationally reactive by using coherence changed my life. I'm very grateful to the practice. This book will teach you teach you HOW and WHY it WORKS when used in your everyday life and with your kids. BUY IT, READ IT, ACT ON IT and GIVE COPIES to all your friends!"
— Kaja Michelson, parent, certified life coach and yoga instructor, Sweden

"As a school psychologist, I've seen firsthand the significant positive effect that practicing heart-brain coherence has on students, teachers, and staff. Adding the skill related to empathy, and integrating these practices as described in *Completely Connected*, can only make that effect more powerful."

— Barbara Hinojosa, Ph.D., Licensed Specialist in School Psychology, Texas

"Rita Marie's work with peace and the Connection Practice has had an amazing impact on members of our community. We have hosted her workshops, had folks go through her facilitation trainings, and even had the opportunity to experience her for two days in Costa Rica! Rita Marie's passion and clarity shine through her heart and words. The BePeace Practice is easily integrated into our spiritual understanding. It helps us heal our human hurts, finds ways to satisfy our human needs while staying centered in the spiritual truth of who we are. It helps us connect with others, develops empathy and compassion, and is a wonderful conflict resolution tool that anyone can learn to use. People are opened and transformed by it almost immediately, and it gives them an ongoing tool to stay that way! I highly recommend Rita Marie and *Completely Connected*. Your community will love her and the practice."

— Rev. Dr. Petra Weldes, Center for Spiritual Living, Texas

To my father, Carl Johnson,
who showed me that life is nothing to be afraid of,
who told me of his own fears and struggles,
and who believed I could achieve my mission.

Dad showing my sister (on right) and me that
grasshoppers are nothing to fear.

Contents

Acknowledgments

The credit for this book belongs to all those who came before me in the science and practice of social-emotional learning, and those who have brought the Connection Practice forward with me for over 10 years. A heart burst of gratitude to:

Life, which brought me the opportunity to joyfully serve in a way I wouldn't have dreamed possible.

Diane Blomgren, friend and fellow practitioner of connection who serves as Director of Curriculum Development for Rasur Foundation International and editor extraordinaire.

Shari Holland, my sister and natural-born peacemaker, who rocked me in Grandma's rocking chair when I was young and is always there for grownup rocking when I need it.

Diane and Lee Brandenburg, whose support made it possible to move forward at key points in the evolution of this work and this book.

Doc Childre, founder of the Institute of HeartMath, and all the good people there, especially Jeff Goelitz, who have responded to my every need over the years.

Dr. Marshall Rosenberg, creator of Nonviolent Communication™, and the many NVC™ trainers who have contributed to the development of the Connection Practice.

Juan Enrique Toro, whose early support gave me the foundation I needed for this work.

Robert Muller, my mentor, who stretched my mind and introduced me to the poem "Rasur."

Elinore Detiger, who broadened my network and supported my work in Costa Rica.

Alexandra Kissling, the Association of Businesses for Development (AED), and Costa Rican citizens who opened the way to a grand social-emotional learning experiment there, along with three Presidents who supported my work in Costa Rica—Nobel Peace Prize laureate Oscar Arias, Rodrigo Carazo and Laura Chinchilla.

The Rasurs—certified coaches and teachers at this time in the United States, the Bahamas, Canada, Costa Rica, Japan, Puerto Rico, and New Zealand—who carry the torch for this mission and bring their collective wisdom to it.

Dee Mayes, our Texas Coordinator, who opens her home to further this work and enthusiastically carries out her role.

Lori Brady and Judy Henry, who developed the U.S.-based Connection Practice curriculum and pioneered the first pilot school in the United States.

Rasur Foundation International and Rasur Foundation of Costa Rica board and staff members, past and present, Lynne Dowler, Shari Dyer, Leigh Files, Barbara Jones, Eric Kasum, Kaja Michelson, Ann Ranson, Ron Hariri, Susan Beck, Carlos Echeverría, Brenda Kleysen, Luis Diego Soto, Marcia Aguiluz, Marlon Mora, Terrie Rodríguez, Kelsey Visser, J. P. Eason, Dyana Berwin, Julie Vosoba, Shelly Patrick, Nancy Marín, Andrés Jiménez, Maribel Muñoz, Vera Lucía Salas, Sharon Boyd, Humberto Fernandez, John Williams, Paula Castro, and the trainers who worked for the Rasur Foundation in Costa Rica.

David McArthur, whose personal, professional and financial support has often been the wind beneath my wings.

Lisa Nichols, super-skilled social entrepreneur who serves as Director of Communications and Operations for Rasur Foundation International.

Michael and Michelle Deese and Bert Headden for their support in printing the first 1000 copies of this book.

Sam Guarnaccia, who composed the delightful music for the children's curriculum.

Phillip Hellmich, James O'Dea, Emily Hine, Holly Woods, and Isabelle Christiansen with the Shift Network

Daneen Burk, Patricia Reiter, and Cat Tennie, soul sisters, and Andrés Restrepo, soul son.

Neal Carson, long-time faithful friend who has supported my work over the years.

David Elliott, John Elliott, and Jenny Toro, who suffered from a lesson I had to learn.

My dog, Millie, and all the dogs that came before her who kept me going when times got tough.

Deborah Shouse for developmental editing, Kathi Dunn for cover design, Hobie Hobart for book know-how, Graham Van Dixhorn for copywriting, Dorie McClelland for interior design, John Eggen and Jill Cheeks for book mentoring, Jean McElhaney for developing the resource list, and Jude Gladstone Cade for proofreading.

The many people who contributed their stories to this book but preferred to remain anonymous. In those cases, their names have been changed.

Completely Connected

Two Kinds of Intelligence

There are two kinds of intelligence: one acquired,
as a child in school memorizes facts and concepts
from books and from what the teacher says,
collecting information from the traditional sciences
as well as from the new sciences.

With such intelligence you rise in the world.
You get ranked ahead or behind others
in regard to your competence in retaining
information. You stroll with this intelligence
in and out of fields of knowledge, getting always more
marks on your preserving tablets.

There is another kind of tablet, one
already completed and preserved inside you.
A spring overflowing its springbox. A freshness
in the center of the chest. This other intelligence
does not turn yellow or stagnate. It's fluid,
and it doesn't move from outside to inside
through conduits of plumbing-learning.

This second knowing is a fountainhead
from within you, moving out.

—Rumi

1.

From Confusion to Connection

Transforming Lives Through
the Connection Practice®

Two years ago, my friend Stephanie faced a challenge she'll
never forget. Only three months after being hired as CEO
of a small company, she was told that the board members
weren't happy with her and wanted to release her from her
contract. She was stunned. She thought back on her actions
since she'd been hired. Knowing that everyone had been
fond of the previous CEO, who had retired, and seeing no
pressing reason to rock the boat, she hadn't made any rapid
changes. Everything seemed to be going along fine.

What, she pondered, could have happened to create trust
issues between her and the board members? She had caught
wind of slanderous gossip about her and tried to discover
the source of it, but the negative feelings of board members
erupted before she could do anything about it.

After receiving the news she was to be fired, Stephanie
requested a meeting with the board. Having been trained in
the Connection Practice, she was confident she could recon-
nect with the members. Prior to the meeting, she took the

first step by naming her feelings of confusion, hurt and anger and identifying her needs for clarity, fairness and to be seen for who she is. Having given herself empathy, now she was calm, in charge of herself, and ready to engage with the board.

The dialogue began with each board member giving reasons to dismiss her. She listened quietly and responded to each one by respectfully guessing what they were feeling and what unmet needs they were experiencing. This empathic style soon revealed that their perception of Stephanie as a person who abused power had no basis in reality. On the contrary, her skill in honoring other people's needs was obvious to everyone in the room.

Stephanie thanked the board members for their willingness to clear this up. Then one of the board members said, "I have no idea how we got to this place, but I haven't heard anything that would give us good reason for letting our CEO go. I'm embarrassed and frustrated to see this happening." Another board member spoke up, "I, too, am embarrassed and would like to apologize to you." Then, one by one, they apologized and affirmed their desire for her to continue as their CEO.

After the meeting adjourned, Stephanie gave more empathy to the board member, Tom, who had initiated this conflict. As she interacted with him, she sustained heart-brain coherence, an aspect of the Connection Practice that increases the odds that we, and even those around us, will become more insightful. Suddenly, a light came on in Tom's eyes. He exclaimed, "I just realized my reaction to you was actually to a CEO I had trouble with 17 years ago. It has nothing to do with you." He was grateful to be able to release that pain from the past.

Later Stephanie shared, "In learning the Connection Practice, I came to understand how any of us can be triggered by memories. It wasn't hard to find compassion for Tom's trauma. I'm relieved we were able to resolve this situation peacefully and forge a deeper, more authentic connection."

Adults aren't the only ones to benefit from the Connection Practice. Joe was acting out at school. In his fifth grade classroom, he was constantly restless and wouldn't follow the teacher's instructions. After failing a math exam, he went out at recess and pulled a classmate across the playground by her hair. Fortunately, his teacher had been trained in the Connection Practice and she sent him to a Connection Practice course for kids. After arriving at our headquarters for the course, he was punching the other boys and it was hard to get his attention. Before long, though, he'd engaged in the activities and calmed down.

I joined Joe's group in the last exercise of the day and asked him whether he'd had any conflicts recently. He told me about the incident with his math exam and hurting his classmate. I began guessing his feelings around this event. "Were you feeling angry because you failed the exam?" I queried. He nodded. As we dug deeper, I found out he'd failed many exams and I guessed he felt some hopelessness over that. "Yes, that's right," he said. I wondered if he was lonely. "Yes, sometimes I am," he affirmed and his face visibly softened.

I began exploring the needs underneath those feelings—needs for learning, achievement and support. When I touched upon the need for belonging, a big tear slid down his cheek. The empathy that we learn to give in the Connection Practice had hit home.

Then I guided Joe through the steps that would help him move his heart and brain into sync. After a few minutes of silence, I encouraged him to ask himself what he needed to know about this conflict and, with eyes closed, just listen inside. When he opened his eyes, he said, "I could ask for what I need instead of hurting someone." Joe discovered the unmet needs that were driving his violent behavior and realized he could ask for support when he needed it. He went back to his school and served as a Connection Practice mediator, resolving conflicts between students rather than hurting them.

Even professional counselors find that the Connection Practice helps them zero in on how to help their clients. One counselor at Nexus, an addiction recovery center in Dallas, said, "I'm good at reflecting my client's feelings but hadn't focused much on their needs. I needed this awareness." "Such a wonderful way to live," said another.

A participant in another course, Linda, said, "As a psychiatric social worker, I opened up my heart and mind to new knowledge, insight and a practice I experienced as positive and healing. This is a great tool to bring to others."

The Connection Practice has transformed my life and the lives of thousands of people from many walks of life. I can share story after story of success, but until you've actually experienced it, its power is hard to grasp. It would be like trying to explain a cell phone to someone living in the 1800s.

This how-to for joyful living keeps me from getting stuck and saves me from unnecessary suffering. In the past, I'd found myself repeating old reactive behaviors or entangled in unfulfilling relationships. Other times I was floundering without a sense of direction or feeling unworthy. At one point, I couldn't bear to read one more self-improvement book as I wasn't applying what I read.

But once I'd discovered this synergistic approach, elegant in its simplicity and often amazing in its application, life got better and I've never looked back. I'm an imperfect, growing human being. Now I'm able to be vulnerable about my weaknesses while also having healthy boundaries and solid self-esteem. I don't waste much time anymore in being confused or in energy-draining conflicts. After we learn the art of connection, many maladies in our lives begin to melt away—burnout, addictions, hurtful conflicts, lack of meaning, depression and harm to our bodies from stress.

My greatest pleasure is in seeing how the Connection Practice impacts people in many different arenas. Recently Anita Campion, CEO of the Connexus Corporation, a global consulting firm, flew from her headquarters in Washington, DC to California, at her own expense, to make a video on how a Connection Practice course had improved relations and innovation in her company. In the interview with Henry Tenenbaum, retired from KRON TV (an NBC affiliate), Anita explained, "Now my employees are more committed to each other and to the work."

People who attend public Connection Practice courses arrive with a variety of issues. John said, "I've felt separate from others every day of my life, but now this feeling has disappeared." Kathy, who had a brain injury at the age of 23 and is now in her forties, told everyone, "For the first time since the accident, I'm thinking clearly." With tears in her eyes, Selidia shared, "I came here in pieces and I'm leaving in peace."

One observer of the impact of the Connection Practice said, "This method

> This method isn't a cure-all, but it is a cure-a-lot.

isn't a cure-all, but it is a cure-a-lot." For the majority of us, learning how to manage our inner lives is a quantum leap forward in functioning as a human being. Once we make that leap, our relatedness to other people is enriched to such a degree that we're amazed we'd settled for so much less.

The Connection Practice

The Connection Practice is a method of social-emotional learning that unites empathy and insight and achieves extraordinary results.[a] Empathy is attained through a conscious connection to feelings and needs, and insight is accessed through heart-brain coherence, a term we'll explore in the next chapter. The synergy in this partnership maximizes intelligence, builds resilience and enhances performance. The accelerated growth it provides includes stopping stress immediately, releasing negative emotions, maintaining emotional balance, improving relationships and resolving conflicts creatively.

The impact of the process is complex and will be explored throughout the book. However, the basic process is simple:

1. Describe your challenge or celebration.
2. Name and feel your feelings.
3. Name and connect with your met or unmet needs.
4. Guess the feelings of others involved in the situation.
5. Guess the met or unmet needs of others involved in the situation.
6. Access a Heart-Brain Insight using these steps:

   • Quick Coherence® Technique[1]:
     a) Heart Focus—Focus your attention on the area around your heart, the area in the center of your chest.

---

a. The Connection Practice is deeply inspired by Nonviolent Communication (NVC) and HeartMath and, with their consent, draws upon these two trademarked and proven processes. The Connection Practice is not defined as a combination of NVC and HeartMath because its focus is the synergy between empathy and insight rather than their complete processes. To learn more, we encourage our participants to take more training available through www.cnvc.org or www.heartmath.org.

b) Heart Breathing—Breathe deeply, but normally, as if your breath is coming in and out through your heart area.

c) Heart Feeling—As you maintain your heart focus and heart breathing, activate a positive feeling.

- Ask yourself what you need to know and listen for an insight.
- Decide how you will act on that insight.

This practice has been tested with over 40,000 students in Costa Rican schools and is spreading into businesses, nonprofits, schools, universities and faith-based communities in the United States and other countries. These participants have learned how to use the powerful partnership between their empathy and insight to connect more deeply with others and skillfully respond to challenges.

The Need to Be Completely Connected

When I look back on how I came to teach this practice, a memory from my childhood comes to mind. My father and I are walking together on our Missouri farm at twilight, ambling along on the parallel paths made by the tractor tires. As we come up to the creek where the paths disappear, Dad asks me, "What's the best way to have confidence in life?" I tell him, "I don't really know." After all, I'm only 10. He says, "I don't know either but I sure wish I did. I never feel comfortable with people." I feel the anguish of Dad's loneliness and our hearts merge in sadness. The mystery of that unanswered question hangs heavily in the air as we fall into silent step together.

Years later, when my father is 87, we're eating lunch at Luby's Cafeteria in Arlington, Texas. "Dad, what events in your life had the most impact?" I ask. He puts down his fork, his eyes downcast, as if quietly listening to a voice of the past. I can see he's challenged by the question and I wait.

"In my early years, my parents created a loving family. That made a big difference. But I was bullied from the fourth grade on and I never told anybody."

"What?" I'm incredulous. "I never knew that. You must have been so scared and lonely. Tell me about it."

As he tells me, I now understand why my father, who has such natural dignity, struggled to have the confidence to fulfill his life purpose. It's no wonder he was seeking advice from a 10-year-old. Bullying stole his confidence. The Connection Practice could have prevented that or resolved it peacefully.

Bullying is one of the many symptoms that shows up when we're unconsciously crying out for connection. Threat Assessment in Schools,[2] a well-researched guide by the United States Secret Service

> Connection is the critical emotional glue.

and Department of Education, says "connection is the critical emotional glue" and "a central component of a culture of safety and respect." Isn't it odd that connection has been diagnosed as critical to a healthy society, yet we don't educate people on exactly how to do it?

If we want to continue evolving into a kinder world, we must have the emotional safety that connection brings us. When two people are connected, they enjoy a level of trust and rapport. Brené Brown, author of *Daring Greatly*, defines connection as the energy that is created between people when they feel seen, heard, and valued; when they can give and receive without judgment.[3] By sharing her research on vulnerability, and her personal experience of it, she's opened the way to a deeper consideration of how we create connection. We've been yearning for that awareness for a long time. Albert Schweitzer knew we hadn't yet discovered how to connect when he said, "We are all so much together, but we are all dying of loneliness."

The concept of connection isn't limited to connecting with others. We must learn how to connect to ourselves. We're flooded with information about what we should do and have, but receive little instruction on how to connect to our own best wisdom. As a result, many people are caught in an epidemic of distractions that don't offer sufficient meaning and joy. When we don't know how to go inside to fuel our purpose, we cope by filling our time with empty pleasures and painful dramas. It's no wonder that people suffer so much from the downs of life; they're missing the ups that come from truly knowing themselves.

Not knowing how to connect, inside and out, has a great cost to our progress. Individual human potential is wasted and organizations go in circles, mired in confusion and conflict. In business, it impacts the bottom line; in school, it reduces learning; and at home, it can lead to divorce. Between countries, it can lead to war. Not having the clarity to consistently connect keeps us stuck, personally, professionally and globally. It causes needless suffering and impairs our hope for positive change.

Social-emotional skills can be a game-changer in solving these problems, but they need to be so achievable we can apply them whenever and wherever we need them. In practicing my own method, I've attained greater ease in handling issues on the day they arise, rather than taking months, and sometimes years, to resolve them. I want others to succeed at this as well so we won't repeat the negative side of our human history; instead, we'll make history through authentic change. That will only happen when our individual actions are guided by a daily experience of inspired growth that flows from connection with self and others.

Having an Efficient How-To
Makes the Difference

Many people are searching for a way to make a real difference and some feel hopeless about societal change. We can move away from that turmoil because now we have a scalable how-to for connection that's been confirmed by thousands of testimonials and over 10 years of program evaluations.

We have scientific evidence that points to why the Connection Practice works, yet there is so much more to know. I'm not a scientist, but I have the greatest respect for research that helps us understand how our inner lives work. At the same time, we can't afford to wait until there is a complete understanding of how we tick before we apply what we know. As a down-to-earth educator, I took the most basic things science taught me about the heart-brain connection and put them into a practical framework that gets positive results. I'm counting on scientists to help me further explore why it works so well.

The Connection Practice is not an all-encompassing remedy, as no one approach can resolve all problems or capture the infinite mystery of life. And I'm certainly not solely responsible for this method; my work has been built on the genius of others, for which I'm hugely grateful and will share about in the pages to come.

I'll also be sharing the experiences of certified Connection Practice coaches, trainers and curriculum instructors, who are collectively called "Rasurs." The Rasurs have contributed immensely toward achieving the vision we share:

a world where every person practices the art of connection and passes this gift on to the next generation.

The name "Rasur" comes from a story about a devoted teacher in an epic Costa Rican poem.[4] Rasur arrives at a small village and calls the children into a mountain, where he teaches them the art of connection to oneself, each other and nature. This goes on for a week and each evening the children share what they've learned with their parents. Eventually, their village is transformed; they're living at a new level of harmony and creativity. This mythical tale inspired the name of Rasur Foundation International (RFI), the sponsor of the Connection Practice.

Years ago, I didn't realize connection with myself and others was essential for my success. I found substitutes to feed the hunger that lack of connection brings, too much food being my primary fallback. When I was disconnected, I did some things that hurt others, as we all do when we're in that state of ignorance. Today life gets better every time I apply what I now comprehend. In the moments when I forget to do that, I remind myself that it's about connection, not perfection. Then the elements of the skill itself help me quickly learn from my mistakes and move on.

People who've adopted the Connection Practice frequently tell stories that are similar to mine about their learning curves with connection. It takes time to integrate this new understanding and language into our lives. I've included a glossary and book study guide in the back of this book to help with that process.

The Connection Practice isn't the end all when it comes to learning how to be a better human being. With the awareness we're gaining from neuroscience, even the best methods will eventually fade into the past. But let's fully use what we know today.

The Time Had Come

My lifelong dream is that people everywhere will have the *ability* to create a more harmonious and innovative world. To make that dream come true, I needed to find a how-to for developing that ability and applying it in daily life. I wanted to discover a social-emotional skill so workable that it became natural to us. I tried different methodologies in search of that how-to until one day it all came together.

It was 2002—I was 50 years old and, with no income in sight, had recently resigned from a job so I could develop a teacher-training program in social-emotional learning (SEL). Although I'd been exploring this field for five years, I had a gut feeling I was missing something essential. I was daydreaming on a comfy couch in my living room in Costa Rica when the epiphany about combining empathy and insight arrived. I sat straight up, wide-eyed and elated, as my thoughts began to race.

This idea integrated what I'd learned about SEL and came with such power that I knew it would change my entire life. I wasn't ready for that; I literally put my hand over my mouth so the revelation wouldn't leak out. It did anyway and, eventually, I was teaching the Connection Practice at the United Nations-mandated University for Peace in Costa Rica to graduate students from different cultures, religions and languages all over the world.

I continue to teach the Connection Practice and I strive to embody it every day. I was baffled in helping Dad regain his confidence when I was 10 but was able to come through for him in his seventies, after I saw the possibility of living a completely connected life. This book is the story of how that marvel happened for him, for me and for others who have learned the Connection Practice—and I know it can happen for you.

Chapter Summary

1. The Connection Practice is a method of social-emotional learning that unites empathy and insight and achieves extraordinary results.
2. The Connection Practice builds social-emotional intelligence, strengthens resilience and enhances performance by engaging empathy and tapping insights.
3. Empathy is attained through a conscious connection with feelings and needs.
4. Insights are accessed through heart-brain coherence.
5. The Connection Practice can keep you from getting stuck and repeating old reactive behaviors.
6. Connection is the energetic bond you have with yourself or another when you feel heard, seen, and valued.

2.

Heart-Brain Coherence
Leads to Insight

A Discovery in Costa Rica

My quest to find a practical way to work with our inner lives
took me down many paths; I got my degree in psychology,
worked with special populations of children and youth,
absorbed personal growth seminars and served as Chief of
Volunteer Services for the Texas Department of Health. None
of these endeavors, though, surpass the education I got after
I was drawn to the peaceful culture of Costa Rica in 1993.
I just knew I had something to learn from this country. I
followed that hunch and it took me on a fascinating journey,
one that's lasted over 20 years and continues still.

After moving to Costa Rica, it took time to understand
the culture and get my feet on the ground. My purpose
there began to unfold when I founded an elementary school
in 1997 in Escazú, a town west of the capital, San José. I
planned to experiment with social-emotional learning (SEL),
which aims to develop life skills for dealing with oneself and
others. Daniel Goleman's book, *Emotional Intelligence*,[5] had
opened my mind to SEL. I was engrossed with the subject,

as it seemed to be a gaping hole in educational systems. I'd heard that the Institute of HeartMath in the United States was doing exceptional research in this field, so I invited their Executive Director, Dr. Deborah Rozman, to Costa Rica to present a seminar.

Dr. Rozman shared intriguing research about the communication between the brain and the heart, using the term "coherence." According to the Institute of HeartMath, personal coherence refers to the synchronization of our physical, mental and emotional systems. It can be measured by our heart-rhythm patterns: the more balanced and smooth they are, the more in sync, or coherent, we are. It's a state of optimal clarity, perception and performance.[6]

> Coherence refers to the synchronization of our physical, mental, and emotional systems.

Negative emotions, such as frustration, cause us to be incoherent; our heart rhythms become erratic. In this state, we have foggy thinking and often act irrationally. Positive emotions create coherence, which shows up as an even, rhythmic pattern. When we're coherent, we think more clearly and are more insightful. *(See diagram on next page.)*

"Generating a feeling of appreciation in our hearts is often the fastest, most reliable way to get coherent," Dr. Rozman advised, "as appreciation is a positive emotion most people can access."

She suggested that we focus on a precious memory, a time in nature, or on something, such as a pet, that is completely positive as a way to get in touch with the feeling of appreciation.

Positive emotions create coherence because the body is a system of oscillators, which means it has parts that fluctuate back and forth—the brain, heart, respiratory

Heart Rhythms (Heart Rate Variability)

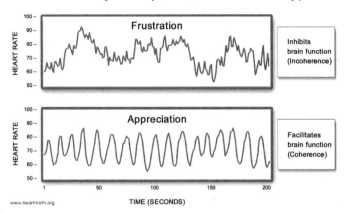

www.heartmath.org   TIME (SECONDS)

Emotions impact our heart rhythms and our ability to think clearly.
(See color illustration on page 249.)
Copyright © 2015 Institute of HeartMath

system and digestive system all have rhythmic movement. These oscillators operate according to a phenomenon called "entrainment," which was discovered in the 17th century by Christiaan Huygens, the inventor of the pendulum clock. When his clocks were in the same room, he noticed that the largest pendulum, which had the strongest rhythm, pulled the other pendulums in close proximity to it into sync. All the weaker pendulums entrained to the strongest one.[7] In the body, the heart is the "pendulum" with the strongest rhythm so it's capable of drawing the other biological oscillators into entrainment with it. (*See diagram on next page.*)

Consequently, a coherent heart can pull the brain into coherence. This state of heart-brain coherence diminishes the reactions of a part of the brain called the amygdala, which is responsible for identifying fearful situations. The amygdala stores memories of these fearful experiences so we can quickly recognize similar events in the future.[8]

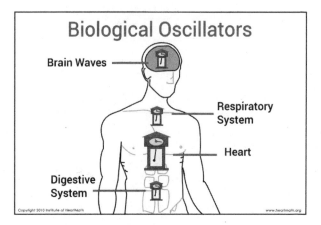

Note that all the "pendulums" are in alignment with the heart.

In the illustration below, a man bitten by a dog when he was a child feels extreme fear as an adult when he sees a dog. When his amygdala receives this information, it moves into a fast reaction. Consequently, he's unable to think the situation through rationally using the slow track of the brain. If this man learns how to become coherent, he can put a stop to this overreaction.[9]

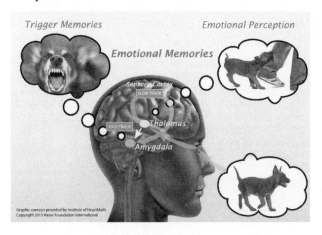

How Emotional Memories Trigger the Amygdala
(See color illustration on page 250.)

Realizing that a coherent heart can pull the brain into coherence, causing us to make better choices, was revolutionary for me. I let it sink in—my heart can help extinguish the irrational reactions of my amygdala, reactions like I have when

> My heart can help extinguish the irrational reactions of my amygdala.

someone hurts my feelings. Since my heart is my strongest oscillator, if I help it become coherent by feeling appreciation, it will help me by pulling my brain into coherence. My heart-brain coherence will override the reaction of my amygdala and free me to choose an intelligent response to stressful situations instead of reacting irrationally.

The Institute of HeartMath discovered the secret to coherence—generating a positive feeling in the heart—and developed a tool based on it: the Quick Coherence® technique.

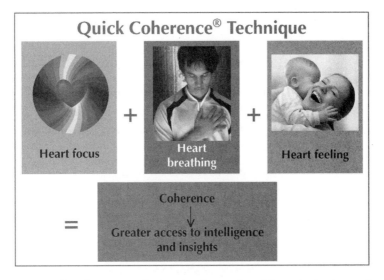

Quick Coherence® Technique

Heart focus **+** Heart breathing **+** Heart feeling

= Coherence
↓
Greater access to intelligence and insights

The Quick Coherence technique is a licensed tool from the Institute of HeartMath. (See color illustration on page 251.)
Illustration copyright © 2015 Rasur Foundation International.

The method consists of focusing on the heart, breathing as if breathing through the heart and then activating a positive feeling in your heart. *(See diagram on previous page.)*

I tried practicing the steps of Quick Coherence and immediately felt a pleasant, peaceful sensation throughout my body. I had lived by the maxim, "Change your thinking and change your life." Changing my thinking hadn't always been easy and now I saw the possibility of a more efficient path: "Change your feeling, and your best thoughts will change your life." By creating a positive feeling in my heart, my brain would operate at its best so I could think clearly, and I'd have better outcomes. Ta da!

After this discovery, I delved further into HeartMath and, over time, became a Resilient Educator® Instructor through their training program. They offer research and a variety of transformational tools that are not covered in this book. We encourage graduates of the Connection Practice courses to take HeartMath training to expand their coherence skills.

How Do We Know Coherence Works?

Research confirms the benefits of coherence. A psychologist at a Phoenix elementary school taught coherence to learning-disabled children. Some struggling fifth and sixth graders were placed in her class for a three-week summer session. The improvement rates were staggering. Even though few reading improvement skills were taught, every student's scores improved, ranging from a two-month jump in reading aptitude to three years' growth.[10]

Other studies confirm students perform better academically after they've learned coherence. One study was done on high school seniors who failed the Minnesota Basic Standards Test, an exam they had to pass in order to graduate.

Passing Rates for High School Seniors
HeartMath Group vs. District Average

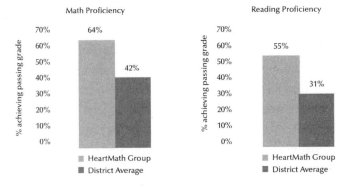

Coherence made a difference in test scores on the
Minnesota Basic Standards Test.
(See color illustration on page 252.)

    All the students in the school district went to a three-week course to learn academic skills that would help them pass, but the HeartMath group also received training and practice in coherence. As the graph above shows, 64 percent of the group that learned coherence passed the math test compared to the district average of 42 percent. In reading, 55 percent of the HeartMath group passed compared to the district average of 31 percent. Coherence was the only difference in preparation between these two groups.[11]

    The following three HeartMath studies have been recognized by the National Registry of Effective Prevention Programs (NREPP[b]) for having met their criteria as evidence-based research.

---

b. NREPP is a registry of mental health and substance abuse interventions that have been reviewed and rated by independent reviewers.

1. United States Department of Education-Funded Study

This nine-school study investigated the effectiveness of the HeartMath TestEdge® program in reducing stress and test anxiety and improving emotional well-being, relationships and academic performance. The primary study involved 980 tenth graders at two California high schools. Some of the results were:

- 75% of the students experienced lower levels of anxiety during tests.
- The test scores improved, on average, by 10 to 25 points.
- Students experienced less fear and frustration, and made fewer rash decisions. They participated more in class activities and demonstrated emotional connection, humor, persistence and empathic listening.[12]

2. Early Childhood Study

An evaluation study on the impact of the Early HeartSmarts® program with preschool children in the Salt Lake City School District measured student growth in four areas: social-emotional, physical, cognitive, and language development. Children in the intervention group showed statistically significant growth in all four areas compared to the control group.[13]

3. ADHD Study in England

In this study with 38 students diagnosed with attention deficit hyperactivity disorder, ages 10 to 12, HeartMath training significantly improved cognitive function and impulse control, as independently measured by the Cognitive Drug Research system.[14]

Science has helped us understand heart-brain coherence and take it seriously. Trying it ourselves confirms that we function at our best when we can sustain heart-brain coherence. In Costa Rica, the teachers in the Connection Practice program regularly guide their students into coherence before exams. María, a teacher at the Yanuario Quesada School said:

> The Quick Coherence technique has become standard practice in my class; the students themselves ask to do it when I forget. I was so surprised to see the effect this tool had on one student. He was aggressive and continually stirred up trouble with his classmates. By becoming coherent, his impulsivity has been dramatically reduced while his attention in class has improved. His progress has been so amazing that he now asks permission to lead the technique in front of the class.

No matter the age, coherence helps us perform better. One of the Rasurs, Ana, coaches students in preparing for California's stringent Certified Shorthand Reporter exam, which licenses them to work as court reporters. Ana shares:

> Taking the exam is a very stressful experience for the students. I offered to coach one candidate, Jaimie, right before her test. She was relieved to have my support because she'd previously failed the exam. The day of the test, I guided her into coherence over the phone. Later, Jaimie relayed that she'd felt a complete calmness, a total connection with her body. She said, "The peace I felt was so present, it lasted through my whole test." She passed the exam.

When individuals are anxious during tests, their brains devote more attention to perceived threats (Will I pass?

What if I don't?) and less attention to the test. This changes when they become coherent; their amygdalae stop hijacking their brains. As a result, they can focus and access their memory and creativity when answering questions.

Using Coherence to Access Heart-Brain Insights

Not long after my first HeartMath seminar, I found myself in a heated discussion with Paula, the Director of the elementary school I'd founded. I wanted to expand the school and Paula didn't, so I suggested we try the Quick Coherence technique to help us calm down. Sitting on my couch, we followed the steps, putting our hands on our hearts as a point of focus, breathing deeply and rhythmically through the heart, and then generating a feeling of appreciation down in the heart.

A few minutes later, I had an insight about how we could expand the number of students in the school and also give Paula the support she needed. She agreed and we quickly moved forward with our plans. I'd

> I'd achieved coherence and then accessed an insight; this moment changed the course of my life.

achieved coherence and then had accessed an insight; this moment changed the course of my life. Thanks to coherence, insights became my constant companions.

Later on, I discovered an article in the *Journal of Cognitive Neuroscience* that helped me understand why coherence leads us efficiently to insights. A research study, *A Brain Mechanism for Facilitation of Insight by Positive Affect*, showed that people in a better mood are more likely to solve problems by insight.[15] Research demonstrated that self-reported positive affect of participants uniquely increased insight before and during the solving of a problem, as indicated by differing brain activity patterns. People experiencing anxiety showed the opposite effect and solved fewer problems by insight. Since coherence in the heart changes an individual's mood to one of positive affect, it's understandable that insights will then flow more easily. Based on this scientific finding, when I combine the resources of my heart and my brain to solve a problem, I refer to my answer as a "heart-brain insight."

When one of the children in our school, six-year-old Gabriel, started hitting classmates and was also hitting his siblings at home, Paula decided to try a HeartMath activity with him that uses three drawings for problem solving. Below is a re-creation of his original drawings.

My Problem	What I Appreciate	What My Heart Says

Gabriel solves his problem by accessing an insight.

Paula began by asking Gabriel to draw a picture of his problem; he drew himself trying to hit his brother and sister as his mother held him back. Then Paula led him into coherence, "Focus on your heart, breathe as if breathing through your heart, and feel appreciation for something that makes you happy." When he opened his eyes, she asked him to draw what had filled his heart; he showed himself playing on a beach with his Ken doll while dolphins swim in the background.

Then Paula instructed Gabriel, "I'm going to lead you back into coherence and, when you're back at the beach, ask what you need to know about your problem." Gabriel quietly listened inside and then opened his eyes in surprise. Paula asked him to draw the answer he received and he sketched someone lying in bed. When asked what this meant, he exclaimed, "My heart said I'm not getting enough sleep! I'm going to bed really late and my mom doesn't know it. When she wakes me up in the morning, she shakes my leg a little bit. It makes me so mad that I'm mad all day long."

Gabriel willingly made a change in his bedtime routine, the violent behavior disappeared, and he was able to concentrate on studying. Before long, he taught himself to write a newsletter on the computer. When his parents witnessed him standing on a street corner, trying to sell his first newsletter, they realized Gabriel was a transformed boy.

This young boy's wisdom is both simple and profound. He learned to get enough sleep, but his most memorable discovery was his ability to access insights for resolving life's challenges.

The Art of Inner Vision

Insights can serve us in every arena of life, including breakthroughs that move humanity forward. Many great scientific discoveries relied heavily on intuitive insights. The Physics Intuition Applications Corporation shares:

> Intuitive discoveries seem to occur when there is
> a strong emotional focus and intention to solve
> a specific issue. A good example of the need for

emotion and focus concerns Archimedes. While visiting the baths, Archimedes suddenly awoke to a principle that would enable him to measure the volume of an object based upon the amount of water it displaced.

At the time he had been wrestling with a royal problem. The ruler Hiero suspected he had been cheated by the goldsmith who had crafted his crown. Archimedes' job was to determine the volume of the crown, so as to learn, from its weight, whether or not it had been made of pure gold. The Roman architect Vitruvius recounts the eureka moment of Archimedes' discovery:

When he went down into the bathing pool, he observed that the amount of water which flowed outside the pool was equal to the amount of his body that was immersed. Since this fact indicated the method he needed, he did not linger, but moved with delight. He leapt out of the pool, and going home naked, cried aloud that he had found exactly what he was seeking. For as he ran he shouted in Greek, "Eureka! Eureka!"[16]

Could it be that Archimedes became coherent as he anticipated a warm, soothing bath and this emotional state facilitated his epiphany?

Becoming coherent and asking what we need to know about an issue doesn't mean we throw out the normal functioning of the intellect. An insight simply presents more information than was previously available. Then our intellect can apply that knowledge. In Gabriel's case, his insight was a fact that had been hidden from view: *I'm not getting enough sleep.* Then his intellect put this awareness to work in his life.

Albert Einstein called the intuitive mind a sacred gift and the rational mind its faithful servant.[17] In practicing coherence, we have both of these aspects of mind at our disposal. This makes it possible to achieve the goal of critical thinking, which is to distinguish clear thinking from unclear thinking through a disciplined process of gathering and evaluating information. The National Council for Excellence in Critical Thinking states that information is "gathered from or generated by observation, experience, reflection, reasoning or communication, as a guide to belief and action."[18] Accessing insights is simply a methodical form of reflection that supports that thinking process. If we don't learn to access the deeper thinker within us, we tend to remain externally focused, which can cut short our human development.

When first learning to listen for a heart-brain answer, I couldn't easily identify which were my intuitive thoughts. Over time, I learned one essential distinction: insights never have a critical tone. Intuitive answers reflect neutrality. Remember Gabriel's insight was "You're not getting enough sleep" rather than "You shouldn't be such a bad boy." If the answer that comes through doesn't have a caring, objective tone, you're on the wrong track.

Another distinguishing factor is that, like Archimedes, after getting in touch with an insight, there are often positive feelings that follow, such as delight, surprise, awe, joy and deep contentment. Most everyday problem solving doesn't bring us that same intensity of positive feelings.

When facing problems, we tend to focus on one perspective and get attached to it, while insights move us into a bigger picture. Imagine you're seeing a bird flying in a blue sky. In that image, I'm guessing you zeroed in on the bird and didn't pay much attention to the sky. That's the natural way our minds work when we're solving a problem or getting a need met; we tend to zero in on one strategy. When we choose the alternative of achieving coherence and asking ourselves "What do I need to know?" we'll find ourselves in the "sky" of all possibilities. Then we can listen inside for the most helpful idea to emerge.

When I'm inwardly listening for an insight, it's similar to when I want to hear someone who is soft spoken. Everything in me becomes quiet so I can hear that person; I'm attentive and expectant, but not straining to hear. The reward of my inner listening is that words come to me, usually in one clear, short sentence. That's my way, but listening to the whispers in our hearts doesn't work the same way for everyone.

One Rasur, Donna, shares how insights come to her:

> Messages come to me in pictures rather than words. One day I asked what I needed to see about welcoming new people to my church. The visual that came was a snail in a brightly colored forest. I wasn't sure what this meant until I told a member about this image. She said she was a "snail" when she first attended. She would poke her head out and then retreat back into her shell. The brightly colored forest is the magic of our spiritual community. We're developing a welcoming program and this insight will help us feel into the experience of the new person.

A Range of Answers

Insights deliver a spectrum of answers that can range from a subtle shift in our feelings about the issue to clarity about our life purposes. Then, when we put that answer into

action and it turns out well, we're motivated to keep return-
ing to that deep well of inspiration.

I experienced that motivational cycle back in 1999. My
work in Costa Rica came to an unexpected stop and I was
deeply discouraged. I went back to Austin, Texas, to reno-
vate my home there after it had been severely damaged by
tenants. After fixing it up like new, I stood silently in the
lovely, empty living room and made a quick decision to live
in Austin again, where life had been so much easier.

I called my husband in Costa Rica and he agreed to
move back to the States. That night I remembered that I
hadn't listened for an insight about this issue. I closed my
eyes and placed my hand on my heart to help me focus
there. Soon I was breathing deeply and filling my heart
with appreciation. I quietly listened inside and the words
were clear: *It isn't time to leave Costa Rica.* I had no idea
why it wasn't the right time to leave, but I changed my
plans. Now I know my most meaningful endeavors in
Costa Rica were yet to come. From experiences like this,
I realized my impulsivity could lead me astray. Over time,
the rewards of my insights taught me to seek that wisdom
before making any important decisions.

Insights sometimes come to us in dreams. By chance, I
discovered that bedtime coherence improves the odds of
having a revealing dream. In 2001, I was working many
hours of overtime as a Program Officer at the University
for Peace. Then, Rodrigo Carazo, former President of Costa
Rica and founder of the University for Peace, asked the
university to sponsor an original musical based on the poem
"Rasur" and asked that Carman Moore, a New York com-
poser, be hired to write the score.

The University for Peace agreed to this request and
assigned the production of the musical to me, since I had

founded the Rasur Foundation and my first book, *The Return of Rasur*, had been inspired by the poem. I was thrilled at this unusual turn of events and recruited a young man, Andrés Restrepo, as the manager of the project. Soon the Costa Rican Ministry of Culture's dance company and youth symphony had agreed to participate and we'd secured the largest theatre in Costa Rica for the performances. Although I was highly motivated, when the responsibilities of the musical were added to my heavy work load, I became exhausted.

One evening I went to bed early and I moved into coherence before falling asleep. Before long, I had a vivid dream where these words came: *You've been trying to do too much. Just pay attention to Rasur and everything will work out. Have you got it?* When I woke up, I knew I would resign from the University for Peace in order to produce *Rasur* and then move forward with my own work—and I did.

As a result of that decision, I was able to develop the Connection Practice and, in 2010, I began teaching it as a credit course to the graduate students at the University for Peace. According to Vice Rector Amr Abdalla, the Connection Practice is one of their most highly rated courses. That would not have happened if I'd held on to the security of my former job.

Now if I'm struggling with a problem, I get coherent before falling asleep at night and I ask for a dream that will help me understand what to do. Sometimes the answer comes in the form of a dream; other times I'll have a very clear insight just as I'm waking up. By getting coherent at bedtime, and setting an intention to receive an answer, inner static recedes and we increase the odds that an insight will show up by morning.

Insights help us interpret our dreams as well. By 2012, my life had become a whirlwind of courses across the United

States and I was feeling a bit homeless. While staying with friends, I dreamed I owned an apartment complex. When I woke up, I felt convinced I had an apartment complex if I could just remember where it was. When I got coherent, I realized my "complex" was made up of the bedrooms of my many caring hosts; I actually had a huge U.S. home!

Sometimes an answer may come as "wait"; then it's a matter of timing. Other times an answer doesn't come at all but may pop into your mind a bit later. Or an answer may come through without consciously formulating a question. I had a powerful insight when I was 10 years old—in the same year that Dad sought my advice. It was a humid Fourth of July and we'd eaten our fill of watermelon. My sister, brother and I were sitting on the front porch of our farmhouse, waiting for it to get dark so we could shoot off fireworks. I felt restless— there was something burning inside me but I wasn't sure what—so I went for a walk down our country road.

As I walked along, the sun was setting and the sky filled up with glorious streams of light and breathtaking colors. I was thunderstruck with the beauty of it and, moments later, I felt deeply peaceful. Then a whisper inside my heart surprised me: *You will work for peace.* I never forgot those words—they answered a question I hadn't yet articulated—but I didn't know what to do with them. The idea of creating a more peaceful world seemed right, but I wasn't attracted to politics, protesting, or finding a guru. I just wanted to learn how best to live. Years later I realized my appreciation of the sunset had spontaneously moved me into coherence, which made it possible to hear that thunderous whisper. I also realized my way of working for peace was in teaching connection. Sometimes it takes hindsight to fully understand an insight!

Not every answer will make your heart sing. I've received

answers I didn't like. Once I was interested in a relationship with a particular man and wondered what I needed to know. To my dismay, the answer was: *Let it be a mystery.* It was a wise answer, as having certainty early on in a relationship can take the sizzle out of romance, but I still felt disappointed. Now I've learned to be patient, hold my question with curiosity and know that the answer will be in my best interest. I don't get epiphanies every time. The striking examples I've shared are to impart what's possible, yet often my answers come simply as a happier feeling or a reinforcement of a previous awareness.

At times, people who haven't yet tried to access their best intelligence say to me, "You can't expect people to be able to access insights just because you can." In over 10 years of teaching coherence and helping people learn to listen inside, I've encountered only a handful of people who didn't have some success at it. Those who find it difficult to access an insight can just practice coherence, as it improves overall thinking. We don't have to access a specific insight to enjoy that benefit.

Since human beings are fallible, insights and our ability to act on them are subject to error as well. Even though we're seeing a bigger picture of a given situation, we still may not see enough to prevent us from making an error. One day I had an inner message to stop moving forward with a small surgery. Consequently, I decided to get a second opinion about the necessity of this surgery. The second doctor encouraged me to continue with the surgery with the first doctor. I thought perhaps my insight was just a reflection of my nervousness and I decided to move ahead. While I was unconscious during the surgery, the doctor made a decision that had a horrendous cost to me and I realized the insight had been completely accurate. I wished I'd taken it more seriously, but I didn't have enough conviction to stand against the expertise of two doctors.

Other times we may mistake a fantasy for an insight, or we misinterpret an insight or we act on an insight without thinking it through completely. At this point, the art of inner vision is not a science. Yet we know tapping that intelligence is definitely going to put us in a better position than not doing so. Research shows us the odds are in our favor when we're coherent and looking for our best answers. This leads us to have a healthy respect for our insights—they help us look beyond appearances to deeper truths and avoid compulsive decisions driven by our fears.

Relying on insights fortifies our positive expectations. We're constantly bombarded with troubles and violence in the media, so our attention can easily become magnetized to the "dark side." When we know there's a ready alternative for dis-

> Relying on insights fortifies our positive expectations.

covering life-affirming ideas, it's easier to process distressing stimuli without getting sucked into a downward spiral.

As we come to trust this process, it's easier to live in the present; it becomes clear that we don't need to have everything figured out in advance. Insights give us the best answer for a given situation at a particular moment in time. Then we can put our intellects to work in affirming and carrying out the new idea. It takes practice but it's so uplifting!

The Essential Pause

We human beings are notorious for reacting without thinking in ways we often regret. We may have learned to stop and count to 10 in an attempt to control our reactions.

That approach was certainly better than nothing; however, coherence is superior to that old remedy because it uses the power of the heart to pull the brain out of a reactive mode. If we've practiced coherence regularly, it will efficiently come to our rescue when we've been triggered into "fight or flight." A Rasur named Sharon explains, "With coherence, I'm able to pause more now and take an emotional step back before responding to a stressful situation. The more I practice this, the more it becomes a habitual behavior."

During a pause, we can make a conscious choice to shift out of negative emotions, which is so liberating. A University for Peace student put it this way, "After I finished the steps of coherence, it seemed like I'd spit out the toxin I've been carrying since long ago." Viktor Frankl, author of *Man's Search for Meaning,* summed up the value of a pause when he said, "Between stimulus and response, there is a space. In that space is our power to choose our response. In our responses lie our growth and our freedom."[19]

For coherence to become the automatic go-to when we're inundated with negativity, it helps to have practiced with only one image or memory. We won't want to take time to figure out what to appreciate in a highly stressful moment. I began learning coherence by repeatedly using my dog, Shanti, as my object of appreciation. My heart and brain came to know that pathway well, so less time was needed to pause and stop my reaction.

When I first learned the steps of coherence, I didn't put much attention on the

Shanti and Me

second step, heart breathing. Over time, I realized the power of taking a deep, belly breath and drawing it upward, as if breathing through the heart. This type of rhythmic breathing quickly relaxes us, moves us toward coherence and brings us into the present. Now I encourage everyone who is new to this method to take full advantage of the second step and, consequently, they have greater success at pausing to get coherent.

After I learned coherence, HeartMath developed emWave™ software for measuring it and learning to achieve it. You simply put an ear sensor on, plug it into your computer and view your heart rate variability on the screen. The software indicates whether you're in low, medium or high coherence and gives you a score at the end, based on the percentage of time you were coherent. It also has games that reward you for spending more minutes in coherence. This makes it fun and easy to learn this essential skill that leads to insights. HeartMath has also adapted the software for use on iPhones; it's called Inner Balance.[c]

The more positive our feelings are throughout each day, the more coherence we experience and the more resilience we develop. Some people move into coherence when spending time in nature or with animals; for others it may be music or watching funny videos on the internet. We can deliberately increase the stimulants of positive feelings in our lives so we're fortified for those moments that aren't so positive.

If you've ever gone on a camp retreat, you can probably remember how it felt to be immersed in nature and fun activities. You may have noticed that insights seemed to flow more naturally and been motivated to write them down. If so, you were probably experiencing coherence.

---

c. To order these products, go to "Get the Habit Going" on page 215.

After the retreat, you may have felt refreshed and ready to jump back into the normal stream of life. That's the resilience that is the natural aftereffect of coherence.

The Fringe Benefits of Coherence

I took further HeartMath training from my friend David McArthur, previously a Director at the Institute of HeartMath. One morning I was scheduled for a training session by phone, but Shanti was dying of kidney failure. I wanted to cancel but David offered to help me through this heartbreak. He let me cry but also helped me return to appreciating Shanti. As a result of his coaching, I'm so connected in my heart to Shanti, it's as if she's alive. I'm not in denial of her death, but I have only joy in remembering her. I've continued to use this approach when I experience losses; it's one of the fringe benefits of learning coherence.

Now I use my new dog, Millie, as my focus for appreciation. When my father was in tremendous pain in the hospital, and I couldn't find a way to relieve that pain, I came home after visiting him and collapsed on the sofa. I was super stressed so I hooked myself up to the emWave to motivate me to get into coherence. Sure enough, the emWave indicated I was in low coherence.

But before I took the first step of Quick Coherence, Millie jumped up on the sofa beside me. As I looked at her, the emWave registered that I had spontaneously moved into high coherence. That's the benefit of practicing over and over with one thing that's completely positive

Millie, My Coherence Queen

and easy to appreciate—it comes back with ease when you need it most.

After feeling appreciation for a chosen subject for a few minutes, it's natural to want to move on. When that happens for me, I move from Millie to other dogs I've loved, keeping my focus down in my heart. Being prepared with things to appreciate is a sure way to sustain coherence longer, which brings us peace in the face of daily stress.

A Rasur, Michael, uses a similar method. He relates:

> I try to swim for half an hour several times a week. I had huge resistance to doing those laps. As soon as I was in the water, I would start thinking about stopping early. Then I tried the Quick Coherence technique while swimming. My easy-to-appreciate focus is the night sky, full of sparkling stars. I do all back and side strokes, so it wasn't a stretch to feel like I was taking in the sky. Images of the tropics began to come to me. Soon, I had a grinning dolphin swimming by my side. And I was grinning, too. The swim time seems to go much faster now.

Speaking of grinning, when I coach people on the emWave who are struggling to get coherent, I ask them to smile and they often move into high coherence. There seems to be a reciprocal relationship here—when our face smiles, our heart tends to move into coherence, and when our heart is in coherence, we feel like smiling.

As each of us masters coherence, we're able to teach others. Gloria had been diagnosed with Lou Gehrig's disease, an illness that leads to paralysis and respiratory failure. She was understandably scared of suffocating. Her daughter, Gillian, asked if I'd work with her mother on this. I taught Gloria the Quick Coherence technique and started her off on the emWave so she could get the feedback that would help her learn rapidly. Gillian tells me coherence made a remarkable difference in Gloria's state of mind at the end of her life.

Along with all these benefits, coherence reduces cortisol, the stress hormone that increases blood pressure. A study on the impact of coherence showed "coherence had significant physiological benefits including reduced cortisol levels" which in turn reduces blood pressure.[20]

Reducing cortisol also prevents the facial wrinkles that come from stress. Cortisol disrupts the formation of new collagen. When you consider what exactly a wrinkle is—a weakening and lessening of collagen and elastin fibers in the skin's dermis—it's easy to understand how stress can directly cause wrinkles.[21]

But no matter how good it is for us, getting coherent must flow from pure choice; otherwise it becomes one more "should." Once we've found a willingness to embrace this state of being, we'll want to notice which of our habits contribute to coherence and which ones don't. I stopped drinking caffeine when I realized the detrimental effect it had on my coherence. On the other hand, dancing to golden oldies, sitting in my mango garden in Costa Rica, and walking with friends all add to my coherence.

Finding Our Hearts

When I presented a workshop at a conference in Vancouver, Canada, I asked for a volunteer to help demonstrate the emWave software. Volunteers for this task have to be willing to let everyone see their heart rhythms on a big screen. Often the volunteers will have difficulty getting coherent because they feel vulnerable in front of an audience.

This time, the volunteer was 100 percent in high coherence during the session. Afterwards, I asked her how she'd done that. She explained, "My family was abusive and in constant crisis. I learned, on my own, how to achieve heart coherence and that's how I survived it."

As this woman demonstrated, coherence makes us strong and builds a deep sense of self-confidence that enhances our performance in every arena of life. It has empowered me to replace stress and fear with heart-felt appreciation that leads to insights and joy. Joseph Campbell, mythologist and author, said, "Find a place inside where there's joy, and the joy will burn out the pain." Imagine how your life would change if you learned to generate coherence, access insights and live from that joy!

Chapter Summary

1. Positive emotions create coherence, which leads to clearer thinking and insights.
2. A coherent heart can bring the brain into coherence.
3. Coherence reduces the reactions of the amygdala, the brain's center for storing memories.
4. The Quick Coherence technique consists of heart focus, heart breathing, and heart feeling of a positive emotion such as appreciation.
5. Insights are objective and are often followed by feelings of delight, surprise, awe, joy and contentment.
6. Insights give us the best answer for any given situation at a particular moment in time.
7. Insights may not arrive right away or be the answers you want to hear.
8. You can build a reservoir of coherence.

3.

Naming Feelings and Needs Leads to Empathy

A Different Way of Communicating

Coherence and the insights that flow from it were revolutionary for me, but I was still missing a crucial piece in my personal growth. When I had negative feelings, I couldn't always find the desire to get coherent or look for an insight. My feelings were demanding to be heard and I didn't want to suppress them, sugarcoat them or express them in ways I'd regret. This confusion over what to do with my feelings sometimes left me speechless during conflicts. I wanted to be more socially-emotionally intelligent in using language, so I kept my eyes open for someone who could teach me that skill.

Back in 2001, I was plowing through emails in my job at the University for Peace and a message caught my eye. Sura Hart, a trainer certified by the Center for Nonviolent Communication™ (CNVC), was coming to Costa Rica and wanted to meet with anyone interested in NVC. I'd heard of this method, developed by Dr. Marshall Rosenberg, and was curious about this "language of compassionate communication." I set up a meeting for Sura with a handful of people.

Upon Sura's arrival at the campus, I gave her a tour. She put me right at ease and soon I found myself leaking frustration about the limitations of my job. Sura listened and then replied, "It sounds like you're feeling impatient and discouraged because you want to contribute in a meaningful way and you'd like some ease in that process. Is that right?"

"That's right!" I exclaimed, feeling a big "ahh" of relief at being heard and understood. I thanked Sura for helping me get in touch with myself. She explained that NVC had taught her how to guess what someone is feeling and needing, which connects us empathically.

That was a light bulb moment for me—identifying feelings and universal needs leads to empathy, a skill I'd valued but hadn't known how to develop. In just a few minutes, this simple approach had made me more self-aware. Later, I listened to Sura's presentation and learned what I now call "Being Human 101."

- My negative feelings result from a perception of an unmet need.

- My positive feelings result from a perception that a need has been met.

Feelings are simply information; they're neutral and therefore not good or bad. However, as a way to understand their relationship to needs, it's helpful to refer to them as "positive" or "negative." We don't want to judge or suppress our negative feelings; they're valuable signposts for getting in touch with needs. Once we name a negative feeling, we're on our way to understanding it, releasing it and being able to think more clearly. That happened for me when Sura guessed my feelings of impatience and discouragement.

She had also respectfully guessed my needs: contribution, meaning and ease. These are universal needs that all human beings share and she'd tuned in to what I was longing for. The moment my needs had been named, they began to feel more like resources. I found myself savoring the words "contribution, meaning and ease" and some new ideas began to surface about how to meet them.

Learning the Vocabulary of Feelings and Needs

Soon after my encounter with Sura, I took a nine-day NVC course with Marshall Rosenberg in Puerto Rico, which immersed me in this transformative teaching. NVC puts our focus on the moment-by-moment flow of our inner lives, coupled with the dialect of our common human experience—universal needs. Relating to ourselves and others from this basis gets us to the heart of matters and elicits our compassion. Consequently, conflict is a creative opportunity rather than something to be feared.

NVC has much more to offer than will be presented in this book. Its richness is not fully addressed in Connection Practice courses, so our graduates often seek out NVC courses afterwards. On the other hand, NVC trainers also attend Connection Practice courses. This friendly collaboration has resulted in greater mastery of social-emotional skills for many people. You can find a list of journal articles and dissertations documenting the positive benefits of using NVC at www.cnvc.org.

There are four steps to Nonviolent Communication:
1. Observation
2. Feeling
3. Need
4. Request

> Universal needs are the heart of the NVC model.

All four steps of NVC are valuable, but universal needs are the heart of the model. Consequently, in the Connection Practice, we zero in on feelings and needs, as that is the essence of empathic language. Below are lists of feelings and needs that are used in Connection Practice courses.

Feelings When Our Needs Are Met

adventurous	enthusiastic	moved
affectionate	excited	optimistic
alive	fascinated	peaceful
amazed	free	playful
appreciative	fulfilled	pleased
calm	glad	proud
centered	grateful	relaxed
comfortable	happy	relieved
compassionate	hopeful	safe
confident	inspired	satisfied
content	interested	strong
curious	intrigued	surprised
delighted	joyful	thankful
eager	lively	thrilled
encouraged	marvelous	touched
energetic	motivated	trusting

Feelings When Our Needs Are Not Met

afraid	bored	disappointed
angry	bothered	discouraged
annoyed	concerned	disgusted
anxious	confused	dismayed
ashamed	depressed	distressed
bewildered	desperate	drained

dread	irritated	shy
embarrassed	jealous	sickened
envious	lazy	stressed
exasperated	lonely	surprised
exhausted	lost	suspicious
fearful	miserable	tense
fed up	moody	terrified
frustrated	nervous	tired
furious	numb	torn
grumpy	overwhelmed	uncertain
guilty	pessimistic	uncomfortable
hesitant	regretful	unhappy
hopeless	reluctant	unsafe
horrified	resentful	unsatisfied
hostile	sad	unsure
hurt	scared	upset
impatient	sensitive	vulnerable
insecure	shocked	worried

Needs and Values List

acceptance	celebration	contribution
achievement	choice	cooperation
acknowledg-	clarity	creativity
ment	closure	dignity
adventure	comfort	ease
affection	communication	emotional
appreciation	community	safety
authenticity	compassion	empathy
autonomy	confidence	empowerment
balance	connection	equality
beauty	consideration	exercise

fairness	nutrition	self-esteem
freedom	order	self-expression
friendship	participation	sexual
fun	patience	expression
growth	peace	shared reality
harmony	physical	solitude
health	security	space
help	play	stability
honesty	power in our	success
hope	world	support
humor	privacy	to belong
independence	progress	to be heard
inspiration	purpose	to have our
integrity	reassurance	intentions
intimacy	recreation	understood
justice	reliability	to matter
knowledge	respect	to be seen for
learning	rest, sleep	who we are
leisure	safety	trust
love	self-acceptance	understanding
meaning	self-apprecia-	well-being
mourning	tion	
mutuality	self-determina-	
nurturance	tion	

Like many people, I wasn't comfortable at first with emphasizing my needs. My upbringing had convinced me I didn't *need* anything. When I looked deeper, though, I found when I don't acknowledge needs, I tend to unconsciously grab food to meet them. Many people deny they have needs, believing that acknowledging their needs would be selfish or make them vulnerable. Yet they often hurt themselves and others as they strive to meet their needs in unconscious or indirect ways, such as sarcasm, self-pity and avoidance.

I saw this pattern in a minister who aimed to please everyone and hadn't yet learned to stay connected to his own needs. He resorted to lying to get his needs met, which ultimately devastated his church. This tragedy could have been avoided if he'd been able to acknowledge and communicate his needs. This skill is so needed by those in service occupations, yet it's rarely taught.

Most of us have a poor vocabulary when it comes to expressing our feelings and needs. After realizing this, I had decks of 48 feelings cards and 48 needs cards printed and I trained a team in how to use them in giving empathy.

These trainers took the cards to a local fair one weekend and laid them out on tables in our tent. Then as people came by, we invited them to describe a recent situation that was stimulating negative feelings. The person was instructed to pick up the feelings cards that resonated for them and put them in the blank space in the middle of the table. The trainer would then choose needs cards to guess what was going on for the person and put those in the middle as well. The individual was asked to identify the three most important needs and the trainer reflected this information back in an empathy statement. The reflection would sound something like this, "When your mother said she didn't want you to date Marcos, it seems you felt angry and resentful because you need respect, understanding and autonomy. Is that right?"

The boyfriend of one trainer watched this process all day long but didn't participate. After he went home, he received a phone call from his cousin, who habitually bent his ear with her dramas. Rather than listening with his usual feeling of resentment, this time he was curious about what was really going on and tried guessing her feelings and needs. Voila! The conversation shifted; she gained new awareness and he learned to connect rather than tolerate.

Gaining the skill of guessing feelings and needs serves us both personally and professionally. A friend of mine had been hired to resolve a 10-year conflict between two affiliated organizations and she asked me what I would do in her shoes. I recommended having the two CEOs use feelings and needs cards to name their feelings and then guess each other's needs. She gave it a try and it worked so well, the two men decided to have their executive teams do the same exercise. Afterwards, the two organizations agreed to use feelings and needs cards to resolve any future conflicts.

In intimate relationships, knowing our partner's feelings and needs keeps us going strong. A couple, Jim and Alice, were going through a painful breakup. After being led through the feelings and needs cards, Alice realized she needed more fun. On the spot, they began laughing and enjoying each other's company. They've stayed together.

People are usually relieved after expressing their feelings and needs. They're often surprised at how many needs are involved in a situation, and being heard gives them immediate confidence. Then they move into taking responsibility for meeting those needs rather than blaming others for not meeting their expectations.

Dr. Doreatha Fields, founder of the Diamond Community School in Florida, was touched by the experience of her teachers in using the cards with their students:

> Gwendell told me, after she introduced the cards
> to the children, there were "tears and release"
> she'd never seen before. She said both boys and
> girls were positively impacted as they dealt with

past emotions and pain the students said "nobody
ever let me talk about." Karen said the feelings
and needs cards are such a rave, the students ask
each morning "Can we do our cards today? I need
to talk."

We use feelings and needs cards with pictures, called
Kids GROK cards,[d] for children who don't yet read. Karen,
the teacher mentioned above, says she also uses them with
autistic students and any of the children who have limited
communication skills. They can look at the pictures and
find a way to express their feelings and needs, which is so
heartening for them.

The vocabulary of feelings and needs is also used to celebrate positive situations where needs have been met. In one
course, Laurie, whose youngest daughter had just married,
stepped forward when I asked for a volunteer to share something positive. Notice in the dialogue below that guessing
feelings and needs doesn't have to sound mechanical; over
time we learn to integrate this new language into our speech
so that it sounds natural:

> Rita Marie: Tell us a little bit about the wedding.
> What were the moments that filled your heart?
>
> Laurie: It was a beautiful wedding in every way.
> We held it in a garden outside this gorgeous Tudor
> home. We had chairs under the trees and the birds
> were singing. We had friends and family from all
> over the country there.
>
> It was clear to all of us how much in love they
> were, completely devoted to one another. They

d. To order Feelings and Needs Cards or the GROK Cards, go to "Get the
Habit Going" on page 215.

wrote their own vows and spoke them from memory. I'll never forget when Joe said his. . . . He's usually not emotional, and I'd never seen him cry before, but as he spoke of his profound love for Molly, tears were streaming down his face.

Rita Marie: What incredible joy you must have felt knowing that Molly was loved at this deep level and that her well-being was in such good hands. Is that right?

Laurie: Yes, but perhaps even more than that, what I remember is when our older daughter, Kate, sang "The Song of Ruth." It's a song set to the words of Ruth in the Bible: "Wherever you go, I will go. / Wherever you live, so shall I live. . . ." My best friend from childhood had sung this song at my wedding to Tom, Molly sang it at Katie's wedding two years earlier, and now Katie was singing it at Molly's wedding.

After the first time through, Kate asked everyone to join in. It's a simple melody; it was easy for everyone to follow along. As I listened first to Kate's beautiful voice, singing with only her guitar as accompaniment, I was moved to tears. Then when everyone joined in and we sang it together, our voices blending in the gorgeous summer afternoon, it was magical. It felt like we were giving Molly and Joe a communal blessing.

Rita Marie: It seems like you felt so much love as you realized the intergenerational connection and the unity of heart that came shining through that song. Is that it?

Laurie: Yes. Leading up to the wedding, I'd been a little sad about the fact that the ceremony they'd planned seemed somewhat secular to me. My husband, Tom, is a former priest, and my faith has always been at the center of my life. Our shared beliefs have been the foundation of our marriage, and we raised our daughters in a deeply Catholic tradition. But Joe isn't a religious person, and Molly is no longer a practicing Catholic. The order of service followed a traditional wedding ritual; a priest performed the ceremony—an old Jesuit friend of Tom's—and there were the usual readings and such. However no hymns were sung, and it felt to me like something was missing. So when Katie invited us all to sing together, it felt so right, so warm and comforting and beautiful—like all of us were blessing this marriage. We were their community, witnessing and blessing their new life together.

Rita Marie: So it seems you felt genuinely reassured and so alive with the awareness that this moment transcended all differences between you? Does that capture it?

Laurie: Yes, exactly. We'd always been such a tight foursome, Tom, me, and the girls. Maybe because we didn't have any extended family in Texas; it was always just the four of us. For whatever reason, we've always been extremely close. So to have that link between all of us, that moment where we sang "Your people will be my people, and your God will be my God, too" seemed to bind us, across time.

Rita Marie: It sounds like you may have had some fear around losing Molly and this song revealed a shared reality with her that wouldn't change—the spiritual bonds that join you forever. And then you felt the awe of that mystery—is that what it was like?

Laurie: (with tears flowing): Yes, *yes*. I'm just remembering now how I felt this sense of being lifted out of time. My wedding to Tom 33 years ago was somehow superimposed onto Kate and Dan's wedding two years ago and now Molly and Joe's wedding. As if I were in time and outside of time at the same time. It was a blissful moment. Even though Molly is writing her own story, as she must, we are still united by this eternal bond of love.

After this dialogue, Laurie told me that, while she knew the communal singing had moved her deeply, until she received empathy, she hadn't fully understood *why* it was so important. "You gave me a great gift," she said.

With our newfound feelings and needs vocabulary, we can readily meet challenges or get more juice out of our happy moments. It isn't always convenient to pull out 96 cards to process our feelings and needs, so we use the lists provided on pages 48, 49 and 50. Eventually, this vocabulary is integrated into our daily interactions and continually enriches our conversations.

> With our newfound feelings and needs vocabulary, we can readily meet challenges or get more juice out of our happy moments.

We Don't Have to Suffer to Be Empathic

Empathy is often defined as the ability to put ourselves in the other person's shoes, to feel into their experience. NVC introduced the language of feelings and needs to help us accomplish that feat. When I first learned NVC, I was amazed at my new level of connection and spent a lot of time focused on my feelings and the feelings of others. I was more compassionate, but I also noticed a new level of sadness.

Eventually, I realized there's a subtle difference between naming feelings and identifying *with* feelings. When we identify deeply with our feelings as if we *are* those feelings, we risk becoming stuck in unnecessary suffering. Moving on to name and connect with the need usually helps us get past that risk.

Tania Singer, an expert in social neuroscience at the Max Planck Institute for Human Cognitive and Brain Sciences, investigates human cognition, including empathy and compassion. Singer has studied Buddhist monks, who are known for being experts in meditation and compassion. When they watched videos of other people suffering, functional MRI scans of their brains showed heightened activity in areas that are important for caring, nurturing and positive social affiliation. In non-meditators, the videos were more likely to trigger the brain areas associated with unpleasant feelings of sadness and pain.[22]

From this study, I understood why my sadness lingered when I'd identified deeply with my negative feelings or those of people I was connecting with. I now use a technique where I feel my feelings, but I don't become them. When I'm experiencing a negative feeling, I say to myself, *I've*

> When I'm experiencing a negative feeling, I say to myself, I've got mail.

got mail. Then I "open the mail" by naming and feeling the feeling, as well as identifying and savoring the need. If the situation involves another person, I guess what they might be feeling and needing. I "answer the mail" by choosing how I will get my need met. This allows the experience to flow in and out of me. In this way, I'm not tempted to think *I am* "the mail." I have feelings; they don't have me. With this approach, I'm caring toward myself and others, yet I don't get stuck in negativity.

That technique also helps me let go of holding others responsible for meeting my needs. When I say, *I've got mail*, I'm reminded that it's my own perception that's generating this feeling. Then in seeking to get the need met, I keep in mind that, although people contribute to meeting my needs, no one is responsible for my needs but me.

I got to practice this when an organization broke verbal agreements with me and then wanted me to sign an agreement that wouldn't be a win-win. I said to myself, *I've got mail* and I opened the "mail" to discover feelings of frustration, doubt and caution. Underneath those, I found needs for trust, respect, integrity and clarity. I also guessed this organization's feelings and needs; I imagined they felt stressed and worried and needed clarity, understanding, support and stability.

Then it came to me that they were preoccupied with a major transition in their organization, and it wasn't the time to enter into new agreements. I felt a surge of gratitude that we hadn't yet signed agreements that would have been difficult for them to honor. Then I saw how to "answer the mail." I contacted their leader and said, "You can count on my support and you will never regret our partnership. At the same time, I'm not clear about how to move forward, so I'm not comfortable signing an agreement."

He responded, "All right. Can we meet in a month and explore possibilities?"

"Yes," I replied, "I can do that." When I've taken time to feel my feelings without identifying *with* them, and pay attention to my needs, I become more responsible, resourceful and compassionate in meeting them.

A Rasur, Monique, explains how she sees it:

> I was very resistant to expressing feelings and needs, as I come from a background where ruthlessness and a strong will are valued. Now I know my resistance was actually a call to look closely at this part of me. To acknowledge my feelings, without identifying with them, and to express my needs were the ways to walk toward greater peace.

According to the NVC model, all human beings are just trying to get their needs met. Sometimes we do it through tragic strategies that hurt ourselves and others. When we're willing to identify our feelings and our needs, we're far more likely to choose life-enriching strategies.

The "Ahh" of Empathy

Empathy is such a deep human need, yet most of us didn't learn during childhood how to give it to ourselves or others. The relief I felt in receiving Sura's empathy is the most common response people have to being understood. A University of California, Los Angeles research study, *Putting Feelings into Words*, provides a clue to the reason we experience a letting go—an "ahh"—once a feeling is identified. In the experiment, subjects were shown photos of people with negative expressions on their faces as a way to trigger their amygdalae into a reaction. The participants were asked to label the emotion they saw on the people's faces, such as "angry" or "scared," while the researchers measured the reaction of their amygdalae. The researchers found that naming the feelings reduced the amygdala's reactions to the photos.[23] I'm guessing our "ahh" of relief when feelings are named is due to that phenomenon.

Everyday encounters give us ample opportunity to help our fellow man find that relief. One day, I was in a bank line in Costa Rica and I noticed a teller who was typing furiously during each transaction. As this man's anger leaked out, the customers seemed intimidated; I decided to see if I could help. First I checked my own feelings and needs: I felt nervous and wanted emotional safety. Without knowing his situation, I had no idea what the unmet need might be; I decided to give it a shot anyway.

When it was my turn to go to his window, I said gently, "Are you feeling angry?" He looked shocked and scrunched up his nose in a frown, then said "no" but his face broke into a big smile. From then on, he relaxed and our eyes met as we smiled when I said goodbye. That's how life gets richer when we can get the reaction of the amygdala out of the way and get to that "ahh."

In NVC, both feelings *and* needs are identified because they are both important for engaging our empathy. In another study, *The Neural Substrate of Human Empathy: Effects of Perspective-taking and Cognitive Appraisal*, subjects were asked to imagine the feelings of someone who was receiving medical treatment and whose face they saw in a video clip. They were also given information about whether this person's medical treatment had been successful or not. Behavioral measures and the brain responses of these subjects showed that when subjects had a context for understanding another person's needs, it enhanced their empathic responses.[24]

Without any context, it's challenging to guess someone's

needs. If I'd known the context for the bank teller's anger, I could have guessed his needs and I imagine our connection would have been strengthened. That's why the naming of both feelings and needs is so powerful in giving empathy.

Once I realized that identifying feelings and needs is the fast track to empathy, I constantly looked for opportunities to practice. One day, after landing in Miami, I stepped into the aisle of the plane, only to be pushed aside by a young man fighting his way

> Identifying feelings and needs is the fast track to empathy.

to the front. I imagined that he needed to get to a flight on time but I also had some negative emotions. So while waiting to get off the plane, I gave myself empathy: I felt annoyed because I value respect and communication. Simply by naming my feelings and needs, I felt peaceful once again.

Despite this young man's speed, I ended up next to him in a long customs line and decided to give him empathy. I asked, "Are you feeling stressed because you need to get somewhere fast?" His mouth dropped open and he looked embarrassed. "I'm so sorry I've been rude," he said. "My wife is about to have our baby any minute now, and I can't seem to control myself from trying to get home faster." As I grasped the context, I was filled with empathy, just like the study said. We were connected, and we talked on. As we parted, he said, "You remind me so much of my mother." I was so glad I hadn't settled for just feeling annoyed.

Empathy for Every Occasion

The simple skill of naming our own feelings and needs and guessing the feelings and needs of others makes a significant difference in every arena of life. I was especially grateful for this skill after a conversation with my mother. She'd been diagnosed with Alzheimer's and I'd talk to her by phone from Costa Rica. On one call, she was concerned about my sister, Shari, and kept repeating the same words over and over. Feeling a desperate desire to connect, I focused in on her feelings and needs, "Mom, are you feeling worried and upset because you care so much about Shari's well-being and want to see more support for her?"

"Yes, I am," she said emphatically and then was able to move on to another subject.

People sometimes ask if empathy works with individuals who are perceived as scary or tough. I've had several opportunities to test that out. Not long ago, I was invited by my nephew, Ben, to teach a session of feelings and needs to students at the junior high where he works as a teacher. He warned me that this school is in a very rough neighborhood and that the behavior of the students might be shocking. I would have about 40 minutes with the students.

After arriving, I put the chairs in a circle, greeted the students as they came into the classroom and gave each of them a list of feelings and needs. Despite these efforts to reach out, the students were rowdy and disrespectful, continually interrupting, laughing and shoving each other around. I was getting very nervous and worried that this wasn't going to go well. When I started talking, I asked about their need for respect. They didn't seem interested and I realized they'd heard this question as an adult demand. They were right; my question was really about my fear of them and my own need for respect.

Then it dawned on me; their behaviors were about trying to connect with each other. These kids live in a disconnected world of broken homes, parents in prison and depressing situations. Their snippy comments, joking and physical pushing were all ways to collectively connect and transcend that pain. I ventured, "As I see you talking and playing around, I'm guessing that connecting with each other is really important to you. That could be because the world you live in feels really disconnected a lot of the time. Is that right?"

Their heads started nodding. I had guessed right this time. Then I shared a story of "disconnect" from my life— a painful betrayal they could relate to. I asked them to use their lists to guess my feelings and needs. As they did, one of them wrote the words on the board; they were engaged. Ben shared an example from his life too and they did the same for him. Then I asked if anyone was willing to share a situation so we could guess the feelings and needs around it.

I saw Justin's hand go up but his head went down. He said angrily, "My father left us last week." One by one, his classmates started guessing his feelings. Did he feel hurt, sad, lonely, worried, afraid? He just listened, keeping his eyes focused on his shoes. Then they covered the needs: did he need support, understanding, trust, reassurance, communication, connection and love? When they finished, I said, "Justin, does it seem like your classmates understand what you're going through and maybe now you're not so alone in it?" With his eyes half-closed, he nodded and gruffly said, "Yes."

After a respectful pause, another student raised her hand and shared her pain over a friend's hurtful gossip. And then another opened up and then another. At the end of the class, they burst into spontaneous applause. One shouted out, "You did great!" I knew it wasn't me; being heard had opened their hearts and the relief of empathy had inspired the clapping. The students were radiating self-esteem; they had a new skill and had contributed to each other's well-being.

Sometimes when I bring up the idea of addressing feelings and needs in a public school classroom, people cringe and say things like, "The kids won't want to do that" or "That's dangerous because the students will be too vulnerable." My experience has been just the opposite. I have found repeatedly that students are yearning to

> When we deny the most basic aspects of ourselves—our feeling and our needs—and don't teach young people how to safely express themselves, it's far more dangerous.

open up and be real. When we deny the most basic aspects of ourselves—our feelings and our needs—and don't teach young people how to safely express themselves, it's far more dangerous.

These bottled-up emotions result in citizens who either lead lives of quiet desperation, as Thoreau suggests, or sometimes explode into violence to get their needs met. Far too often, we've swept feelings and needs under the rug and called this tenuous state of affairs "peace." Our cultures have taught us to habitually suppress our negative feelings because we didn't have clarity about a safe way to express them. Now we do and it's up to educators to create emotionally safe classrooms so students can learn how to be vulnerable and have boundaries too.

As we improve on our ability to give empathy in many different situations, we discover that written empathy can be as effective as verbal empathy. A minister had received an e-mail from a congregant who accused him of being dishonest with the church's finances. He'd written back asking what she was referring to. She replied, "You know what you've done!" and she copied the national headquarters for that church. The minister asked me for advice and I helped him write his reply to her, "It sounds like you're upset because you need honesty." She wrote back saying, "That's right! You did . . . (thus and so)." Now the minister realized there'd been a misunderstanding and he was able to respond with the facts. She realized she'd been in error and offered to help spread the truth to the rest of the congregation.

Empathy brings our dear ones closer. Andrés, a young man who'd become like a son to me, decided to move to Australia. Later he wrote me about how disillusioned he was with his university there and how distressed he was with his humdrum job. He yearned for a noble life. I wrote him back, guessing his feelings and needs. In NVC, we sometimes use words like "value, long for, yearn for or want" rather than "need," as they can be easier for people to hear.

So I guessed that Andrés was feeling discouraged because he valued meaning, purpose, and living in integrity with his ideals. I responded in a similar manner to his other frustrations. He had no idea that I'd used my newly acquired NVC in my email. He wrote back, "I love you. When I make my first million, I'm giving it all to your work." I don't need to count on that; what matters to me is that our bond can be deepened despite physical distance.

In our relationships, the moment we think we know a person, the relationship begins to die. Empathy moves us out of our assumptions and conclusions, into a depth of understanding that is as dynamic as life. It's no wonder the divorce rate is so high when people haven't been taught how to create sustained, meaningful communication.

> Empathy moves us out of our assumptions and conclusions, into a depth of understanding that is as dynamic as life.

My family certainly lacked those skills. Although the five of us got along and thought we knew each other, we didn't talk frequently and we rarely talked beyond the superficial level. Consequently when I moved to Costa

Rica, my relationship with my sister, Shari, had less and less pizazz in it and it wasn't easy to find things to talk about over the phone.

After I developed the Connection Practice, Shari jumped on the bandwagon and became very skilled in it. Now we have a more dynamic relationship; it's as if a new door opened and we can know each other beyond what is familiar. In this way, we've also discovered how different we are and have faced some moments when our problem-solving strategies clashed. Shari and I got through those times by practicing what we preach, which has brought us to a more authentic, enriched sisterhood.

Once an individual has learned how to give empathy, there will still be moments when he or she falls back into habitual responses, such as giving advice, minimizing a situation or pointing out the positive side of things. These responses are well intentioned and sometimes they're appropriate, but they're not empathy. Those habitual responses convey *our* perspective rather than tuning in to the *other person's* experience. It takes practice to give empathy rather than these types of responses, so we need to give ourselves regular doses of patience and self-acceptance as we learn this new language.

Empathy and Honesty

Empathy is not intended to release people from responsibility for their actions. We can be connected heart to heart with people

> Empathy is the great connector; honesty is the great teacher.

and still hold them accountable. This is where honesty is needed to provide a balance to empathy. While empathy leads to understanding and forgiveness, honesty leads to new awareness. The two are complementary. Empathy is the great connector; honesty is the great teacher.

The problem is that many of us hold our honesty back. In a conflict, if we focus only on giving empathy and don't honestly express our own feelings and needs, we get to feel safe. There is a cost, though, to that safe route, as the other person doesn't have the opportunity to know us or learn from us; we aren't authentic.

Some people think that being authentic means they have license to express their judgments and blame. Not long ago, a man told me he'd asked an obese woman how much more weight she planned to gain and explained that this remark was "authentic and honest." This approach rarely works out well, which is why many of us choose to keep our judgments to ourselves. At the same time, without a clear way to express judgment-free honesty, we stuff our perceptions and often put distance between ourselves and the person in question. When we stuff our honesty, we also risk that it will leak out in dysfunctional ways or cause internal stress that can lead to disease.

NVC teaches us a more rewarding way to interact when we want to express our honesty. By saying what we observed, how we felt and what needs are met or unmet, we take responsibility for our perceptions. Then we have the opportunity to hear how the other person sees it and find our way to mutual understanding.

Several years ago, I became ill and went to four different doctors trying to understand what was wrong with me. Finally I received the proper diagnosis and was astounded that the other doctors had missed it. In hindsight, I saw that none of them, after seeing my symptoms, had suggested the most obvious test. I was upset at my loss of health, time and money and also was concerned this same thing could happen to other patients.

So I wrote to each doctor, guessing their feelings and needs around treating me. Then I expressed my observations, feelings and needs, choosing my words wisely so my letter would have the best possibility of reinforcing our connection, rather than creating fear. Two of the four doctors communicated back to me in a caring way, which I appreciated. I'm guessing the other two may have been able to hear me but didn't respond because of advice they've received about liability. I was all right with that because I'd been empathic and honest in a way that brought me peace.

In the above situation, I modeled one of the most important lessons of my life: when we want to express our honesty, *it's wise to give the other person empathy first*. After making a connection through empathy,

> When we want to express our honesty, it's wise to give the other person empathy first.

honesty will have a better chance of being heard, which is what happened with the doctors. By giving your empathy first, you naturally move into a more compassionate state before expressing your honesty.

Years ago I learned how valuable that lesson is when I presented a workshop to the Central American Leadership Initiative, a group of leaders associated with a U.S. think tank, the Aspen Institute. The workshop was held at the INCAE Business School, known as the Harvard of Latin America. After being introduced, I noticed the 15 powerful leaders sitting at the U-shaped table around me had their laptops on and their cell phones handy. Several kept on working as I started speaking, but I soon had their attention with the feelings and needs cards, that is, except for one fellow. He seemed very busy and paid sporadic attention as the morning progressed.

At the end of the day, this same man came up to me and said, "Thank you so much. You've changed my life today. I wasn't listening much till the end when I heard you talk about putting empathy *first*, and honesty *second*. I've been screwing up my personal and professional relationships all my life because I didn't understand that. Now I know exactly what to do differently." I was happy to hear of his epiphany and, from what I had observed of his disconnection from the rest of the group, this realization seemed to be just what he needed.

Giving empathy first and honesty second works as long as you can do it authentically. If you're too triggered to be present to the other person's needs, you're better off to withdraw and give yourself empathy until the charge is off and you're truly ready to attempt it. When we give our honesty, we walk a razor's edge between communication and blame. If the words we use are empathic, but the tone of our voices implies blame, it's difficult to succeed in rebuilding a connection.

When you know you'll be going into a highly charged situation, it helps to write out the empathy and honesty in advance. You can bring this script with you, and even read from it, if it helps you stay on track. We are all susceptible to slipping into judgments and blame, so this approach helps us avoid saying things we may regret.

In our Connection Practice courses, the participants work in pairs to role-play situations where they've been afraid to be honest. With their new skills of empathy and judgment-free honesty, they practice finding the courage to speak up. We call this "stand-up honesty."

I mentioned that honesty is the great teacher. When friends have the courage to express their honesty to you, it can illuminate your blind spots. An NVC friend came to me one day and told me when I talk, I use too many words and say them with too much intensity. I realized this was true and that this behavior came from a childhood belief about how to be heard. I'm so grateful that he brought it to my awareness as I've shifted it and been more effective in my communication. I'm sure many people knew this about me, but he was the only one who gave me the gift of his honesty.

In Connection Practice courses, we have a favorite way of summing up the dynamics of healthy honesty: When I express my honesty, I hold equally important my need for authenticity, your need for safety and our mutual need for connection. That's the kind of honesty that can move mountains.

> When I express my honesty, I hold equally important my need for authenticity, your need for safety, and our mutual need for connection.

In the Connection Practice, we teach how to express both empathy and honesty. Our emphasis in the introductory course is on empathy; we introduce honesty in the second course. After learning to give empathy, grasping how to express blame-free honesty comes much easier.

Healthy Boundaries

Learning to be more empathic doesn't mean we must give empathy to every person we meet or dive into every available conflict to create connection. We must assess where to invest our energy. In addition, we need healthy boundaries when it comes to opening up to others and holding them accountable for their actions. Brené Brown, in *The Gifts of Imperfection*, put it this way:

The better we are at accepting ourselves and others, the more compassionate we become. Well, it's difficult to accept people when they are hurting us or taking advantage of us or walking all over us. This research has taught me that if we really want to practice compassion we have to start by setting boundaries and holding people accountable for their behavior.[25]

To set boundaries and hold people accountable, we have to slow down enough to be in touch with what's happening, inside and out. As we become more masterful at empathy for ourselves and others, we slow interactions down, get clear on when needs are being met and when they aren't, and follow through with people. This degree of care creates emotional safety, which gives us the courage to be both vulnerable and honest. Once you find how rich life is at that level, you lose your appetite for anything less. Unhealthy relationships tend to fall away and you gain confidence in your ability to have healthy ones.

> To set boundaries and hold people accountable, we have to slow down enough to be in touch with what's happening, inside and out.

Education about Empathy

Education about empathy is spreading. An article by the Greater Good Science Center, based at University of California, Berkeley, reported:

> While teaching empathy in schools isn't a novel concept, the practice has been gaining attention

in the wake of high-profile incidents of bullying and youth violence. Ashoka tried to tap into this momentum in the education world through its "Activating Empathy" competition . . . the crowd-sourced contest received more than 600 entries over three months. The entrants ranged from a high school arts program in China to after-school dance and community sports programs in the United States, all with the stated goal of fostering kindness and understanding.[26]

It's not surprising that empathy is becoming a popular theme because it connects us and sets us free. When we repeat negative feelings over and over again, neural pathways in the brain become super highways to an amygdala prison, a place often filled with loneliness, anger and depression. Empathy sends us out the door of that prison and brings us to life again. When we set our intention for connection, rather than blame or rejection of ourselves or others, any progress is a reason for celebration and any mistake is simply a stimulant for more learning.

Henry David Thoreau said, "Could a greater miracle take place than for us to look through each other's eyes for an instant?"[27] Just imagine how your relationships will be enriched by mastering the skill of empathy.

Chapter Summary

1. Identifying feelings and needs leads to empathy.
2. Negative feelings result from a perception of unmet needs. Positive feelings result from a perception that needs have been met.
3. There are universal needs that all human beings share, needs like contribution, meaning and ease.

4. If people don't acknowledge their needs, they get their needs met in unconscious or indirect ways, such as sarcasm, self-pity and avoidance.

5. Giving advice, minimizing a situation or pointing out the positives in a situation isn't empathy.

6. Empathy does not release people from responsibility for their actions.

7. Empathy first, honesty second.

4.

Empathy + Insight = Connection

The Big Aha

Something else significant happened in June 2002 while I was at the NVC course taught by Marshall Rosenberg in Puerto Rico. When I tried to use my new vocabulary in sentences, I found it difficult to speak the NVC lingo. I'd get tongue tied, worrying I wasn't going to get it right. I knew my thoughts were getting in the way, so I practiced heart-brain coherence to help the words flow.

After a few days of combining coherence with my new NVC, I decided to share this idea with Marshall and the group. I explained, "The perfectionist in me takes the complexity of NVC and turns it into a nightmare. So I've been practicing a technique from the Institute of HeartMath that gets me out of my head and lets the NVC flow from my heart." I led them in Quick Coherence and then used the story of Gabriel to illustrate the big bonus of coherence—insights. Afterwards, a woman who seemed very sad came up to me and said, "You have no idea what that experience did for me. I have a glimmer of hope now."

When I got home, I was brimming with new knowledge, but I sensed there was something I wasn't seeing. I lay down on the couch and my thoughts drifted back on all I'd learned. For years, coherence connected me to my insights, my "ahas." Now naming universal needs was leading me to empathy, where I could connect with myself and others through an "ahh" experience. At last, I'd learned to connect inside and out.

Then my heart jumped as I imagined this: If I applied both empathy and insight to any one issue, the synergy between them would be magically powerful. Synergy means cooperative action; the result is greater than the sum of the parts. The magnified sum of empathy and insight would be able to help people like that depressed woman at my NVC course.

Thus, the Connection Practice was born, and the partnership between empathy and insight became the focus of my life. The diagram on the next page shows the synergy in the Connection Practice that helps us respond intelligently to whatever life brings us.

Together, empathy and insight are a double dose of transformative power.

> Together, empathy and insight are a double dose of transformative power.

Over time, the Connection Practice evolved into three distinct activities:

1. The Connection Process—the steps for uniting empathy and insight to resolve daily challenges and celebrate life

2. The Connection Path[e]—a tool for resolving difficult conflicts with others, or within yourself, through a progressive experience of empathy and insight

3. Connection Mediation—conflict intervention that integrates empathy and insight

---

e. Inspired by NVCDanceFloors.com.

Completely Connected

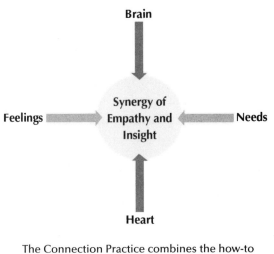

The Connection Practice combines the how-to
of empathy and insight to completely connect us.
(See color illustration on page 253.)
Copyright © 2015 Rasur Foundation International

The Connection Process: A Daily Uplift

After the idea of combining empathy and insight arrived,
I was anxious to try it out in real life. Mary was a recently
divorced woman who came to me for counseling. Here are
the Connection Process steps we used:

1. *Describe your challenge or celebration.*

Mary explained her challenge: "I've started dating again,
and I'm confused about when to say 'yes' and when to say
'no' to the man I'm dating when it comes to intimacy."

2. *Name and feel your feelings.*

I helped Mary identify her feelings—anxious, scared,
confused, vulnerable, ashamed and guilty.

3. *Name and connect with your met or unmet needs.*
   Then we addressed her needs—emotional safety, health, clarity, connection, sexual expression, honesty, self-integrity, self-acceptance and self-empathy.

4. *Guess the feelings of others involved in the situation.*
   We guessed how John, her date, might feel if she says "no" to any form of intimacy—embarrassed, vulnerable, disappointed, frustrated and hurt.

5. *Guess the met or unmet needs of others involved in the situation.*
   We guessed John's needs—connection, sexual expression, emotional safety, clarity, communication and acceptance. As we completed this step, Mary said with surprise, "My heart opened when I realized John's needs are almost the same as mine."

6. *Access a Heart-Brain Insight by using the Quick Coherence technique, then asking yourself what you need to know and listening for an insight. Decide how you will act on the insight.*

I explained the three steps of the Quick Coherence technique to Mary. I asked her to choose something to appreciate so she would be prepared to generate a positive feeling. Then I instructed, "I won't say anything more after leading you into the third step of coherence, as my voice could get in the way of your inner listening. When you feel peaceful from the coherence, ask yourself what you need to know and listen for an insight. When something comes, open your eyes so I'll know you're complete."

Quick Coherence Technique

1. Heart Focus—Focus your attention on the area around your heart, the area in the center of your chest.
2. Heart Breathing—Breathe deeply but normally and feel as if your breath is coming in and out through your heart area.
3. Heart Feeling—As you maintain your heart focus and heart breathing, activate a positive feeling.

As I guided her, Mary put her hand on her heart as a point of focus, breathed deeply and rhythmically and moved into the feeling of appreciation. Then she silently asked herself what she needed to know and listened inside. In a few minutes, she opened her eyes and said, "I got an image of sitting with John and doing these steps to get insights together."

I asked, "What will you do with that?"

Mary said, "This answer is simple and it's doable because I believe John will be willing to join me in this new way of getting to know each other. I feel calm now."

Within an hour, Mary had the clarity she needed to be confident and communicative in dating John. This experience helped me realize this way of working with people was effective. I began to practice the steps regularly in my own life and, later, Mary became a skillful Rasur.

To receive the full benefit of the Connection Process, we encourage people to use a workbook[f] that guides them through the six steps on a daily basis. James Pennebaker, a professor in the Department of Psychology at the University of Texas at Austin, is author of *Writing to Heal.*

---

f. To order this product, go to "Get the Habit Going" on page 215.

His research has shown that short-term focused writing can have a beneficial effect on our health, especially if we are able to flip back and forth from our own perspective to another person's perspective.[28] He also says that people who use "insight" words such as "realize, understand or become" in their writing are more likely to improve their health.[29] From his conclusions, we can surmise that combining empathy and insight is even more powerfully beneficial when written down.

After writing the Connection Process out each morning in our workbooks, moments of stress may come up during the day. We can use the process without

> We take advantage of each part, and we have the whole practice as a foundation for conscious living.

writing it out and it isn't always necessary to repeat all the steps. Moment by moment, sometimes all we need is to give ourselves empathy, or give empathy to someone else, or just get coherent. We take advantage of each part, and we have the whole practice as a foundation for conscious living. Learning the Connection Process is a starting point; our journey with it becomes less formulaic and more profoundly rewarding as we learn to stay in tune with ourselves.

The Connection Path: From Conflict to Peace

The Connection Path is a conflict resolution tool that has the power to resolve all manner of conflicts and heal deep issues, using the synergy between empathy and insight. The steps of the path are laid out on the floor as pictured on the next page. The client who is troubled with a conflict walks on each step of the path with a coach. The other individual in the conflict is usually not present. Someone else stands in for that individual. The path is not a role-play; the stand-in

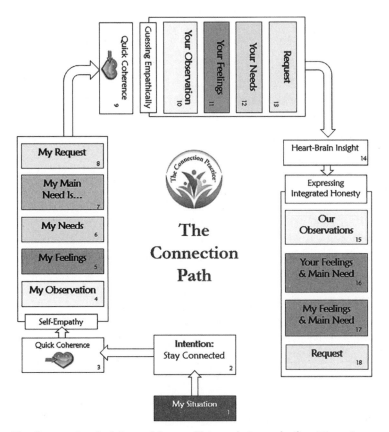

The Connection Path is used for conflict resolution, whether it is an inner conflict or conflict with another person. (See color illustration on page 254.) Copyright © 2015 Rasur Foundation International.

person remains silent, serving only as a set of human eyes and a human heart for the purpose of practice. After walking the path, the client is better prepared to handle the conflict in real life.

To follow the flow of the path, start at the bottom center of the diagram above where you see a rectangle that says "My Situation." Then just follow the arrows.

One of the most transformative moments I've witnessed on the path was with Janet, who was furious at her husband,

Jack. Before starting the path, she explained that she'd suggested they take a summer vacation to Europe. He'd responded, "Are you crazy? You're way out in left field. We can't afford that."

Janet knew they had plenty of money so Jack's comment didn't make sense to her. She said, "Jack never wants to do things with me anymore and our marriage is dullsville. I'm thinking about filing for a divorce."

When Janet explored her judgments toward herself, she discovered thoughts like "Why do I let my husband stomp on my enthusiasm while I swallow my anger? I must have low self-esteem. What's wrong with me?" She also had judgments toward Jack and fumed, "My husband is like a brick wall and I'm sick and tired of pounding my head against it. He never says anything positive anymore. He's just a jerk."

To begin transforming those judgments, Janet followed me as I led her in the Quick Coherence technique. She used a memorable sunrise as her focus for appreciation and her shoulders had relaxed by the time she opened her eyes.

Now Janet was ready to experience self-empathy. As she recalled Jack's comment about the vacation, she felt angry, hurt, sad, weary and desperate. With tears in her eyes, she identified her needs as communication, respect, fun, connection and hope. I asked, "Which need resonates the most for you?"

"Connection," she said. I asked her to bring to mind a time that this need had been fully met with anyone in her life. She chose to remember how connected she was with Jack on their honeymoon.

It was clear that Janet was less charged up and more open now, so I asked if she was willing to practice giving empathy to Jack. "Yes," she said, "I'll give it a try."

The next step on the path involves appreciating something

about the person that you're in conflict with as you do another Quick Coherence. Janet shared, "I can appreciate the fact that Jack has always been a solid breadwinner."

"Okay," I replied. "Let's move into coherence and when we get to the third step, focus on appreciating Jack for his ability to create financial security." Janet closed her eyes to fully engage her heart and, when she finished this coherence, she was ready to practice giving empathy to Jack.

She looked at the man standing in for Jack and offered, "Jack, when I suggested going to Europe this summer, I'm guessing you felt anxious, worried and annoyed because you need autonomy, inclusion, consideration and security. If that's true, I'm guessing that your main need is security."

Suddenly Janet looked startled and said, "Oh my God, I just remembered on our honeymoon, Jack told me he'd been to Europe and never wanted to go back. He didn't tell me what happened, but I'm guessing something scared or hurt him. So when I asked about going to Europe, probably all those old feelings came up. Maybe what he really needs is emotional safety."

Janet was able to access this memory because the steps on the path had taken the charge off the issue and helped her access her best intelligence. I encouraged her to try giving empathy again.

She said, "Jack, when I suggested going to Europe, I'm guessing you may have felt a little fear around that and needed some emotional safety. Is that right?" The man standing in for Jack nodded.

Now it was time for the third coherence on the path, which moves into Heart-Brain Insight. I led Janet into coherence and she silently asked herself what she needed to know. When she opened her eyes, they were filled with tears. "I just realized that Jack's unmet need for emotional safety and my unmet need for connection are the main reasons our marriage is falling apart. I haven't known how to help him feel safe and he doesn't know how to help me feel connected."

Janet had a new light in her eyes as she stepped forward to express her "integrated honesty," so named because it takes into account the needs of both people involved in the conflict, as well as any new insights about the issue.

Janet spoke softly to the person playing her husband, "Jack, when we talked about the vacation in Europe, it seems you felt a little fearful because it reminded you of your need for emotional safety. I haven't known how to help you feel safe in our marriage either.

"At the same time, I felt sad after that conversation because I yearn for the connection that we used to have. I'm willing to spend the afternoon with you, exploring how I can create more emotional safety in our relationship. Would you be willing to spend it with me so we might find our way back to a connection?" Jack's stand-in nodded and gave Janet a big hug.

Janet was amazed at the clarity and healing she had discovered on the path and was ready to go home and try giving her husband empathy.

I've been honored to observe countless other breakthroughs similar to this one. A University for Peace student reported, "As I followed the path, I got some insights that helped me understand the circumstances behind what had happened in my conflict. Those insights were priceless. Forgiveness was never my intention, but it came without any effort. Transforming our hearts from hatred to forgiveness comes along so naturally with this practice."

Often individuals have an "aha" simply by seeing that the path is divided into three sections, three ways of relating that come together as one.

1. all about me (self-empathy)
2. all about you (empathy for the person you're in conflict with)
3. all about us (integrated honesty)

Many people are still living in an "all about me" world; others lean toward self-sacrifice in an "all about you" perspective. The majority of us haven't learned to integrate those two mindsets into an "all about us" perspective

> As people walk the path, each step helps them detach from their judgments and blame.

that honors the need for both individual expression and collective cooperation. As people walk the path, each step helps them detach from their judgments and blame while moving toward a shared reality with the other person.

Once people have learned how to use the Connection Path to work out conflicts with others, they can also learn to use it for resolving inner conflicts. Participants can put parts of themselves on the path that are at war, such as their "critical parent" and "inner child" and bring them into harmony.

I used this method to work on my own healing; I put the inner voice of my critical parent that says "you are the bad kid in this family" in dialogue with the wounded child who suffered from that belief. When I tapped into the needs that the voice of my critical parent was trying to meet—clarity, ease, order and harmony—and discovered the needs of my wounded child for acceptance, support and to be seen for who I am, I found compassion for them both. The insight that arrived was: *The belief you are the bad kid of the family has nothing to do with you—it's Mom's pain that was passed on to you. You can give it back.* And I did—Mom had already passed away, but I silently told her this wasn't my issue and I hoped she'd be able to heal it now.

Connection Mediation: Intervention Brings Us Closer

A Connection mediator builds the connection between two individuals in a conflict by coaching them through the process. The individuals must be educated in the basics of the Connection Practice before beginning the mediation process.

- The mediator leads the two people in the Quick Coherence technique to help take the charge off the issue.
- Person A shares what happened, how she felt and what needs weren't met.
- Person B repeats back what has been shared until Person A feels heard.
- Person B shares what happened, how he felt and what needs weren't met.
- Person A repeats this back until Person B feels heard.
- The mediator summarizes the main needs that have been expressed by each party.
- The mediator leads them into coherence.
- They listen inside for insights and then share them with each other.
- Each party makes a request of the other to provide final closure on the conflict.

One day I was working at our headquarters and heard two women cursing at each other on the patio. I went out to see what was going on. I discovered that these women, who had learned the Connection Practice and were friends, had gotten into quite a fight. Sally had inadvertently broken Christine's vase and then accidentally spilled hot coffee on her and, in recovering from that, had also stepped on Christine's toe. At this point, Christine was screaming, "Get the hell away from me!"

Sally was screaming back, "It's not my fault—it was just an accident!"

I asked if they would be willing to let me serve as a mediator. They agreed and I led them in a long coherence in order to take the charge off the emotions. Then we began the process of getting reconnected by each woman listening to the other's feelings and needs and repeating them back. When we went into coherence, they each had insights that pointed to their friendship being more valuable than anything that had happened. When they made their requests, Sally asked, "Will you let me replace your vase?"

"Yes," Christine replied, "and when you start getting nervous, would you be willing to stop and practice coherence so accidents are less likely to happen?"

"Sure," Sally answered. They were both grateful they hadn't lost their friendship over this incident.

University for Peace students are exposed to various forms of conflict resolution and mediation in their coursework. When they learn Connection Mediation, they are amazed at how identifying feelings and needs, plus coherence and insights, takes mediation to a more powerful level. With this form of mediation, we can more frequently resolve our differences in a way that brings us closer. In our Costa Rican school program, we have trained 424 students to serve as mediators in their classrooms. We want to see kids around the world achieving this skill.

> With this form of mediation, we can more frequently resolve our differences in a way that brings us closer.

Moving Forward with the Connection Practice

As I developed these three activities, I began training volunteers in Costa Rica in the Connection Practice. (We went through several name changes before we settled on SerPaz®, meaning BePeace®, for the Costa Rica school program and the Connection Practice for the U.S. program. For simplicity, I'll use the Connection Practice as I talk about them both.)

By 2004, the volunteers were working in the Elías Jiménez Castro School in Desamparados (which means "homeless" in Spanish), a town south of San José. On the contrary, we couldn't have chosen a better "home" for initiating this work; we were well supported and gained the experience we needed to improve and expand the program.

By 2005, our project won the *Ashoka Changemakers Innovation Award: Building a More Ethical Society*, chosen from 79 projects in 32 countries. Now, our staff members in Costa Rica have trained over 1,500 teachers in 45 schools. More than 40,000 students have been impacted by those teachers, and our staff has directly trained over 4,000 students.

As we implemented our program in Costa Rica, I was heartened by the support of Doc Childre, the creator of HeartMath; Marshall Rosenberg, creator of NVC; and their organizations. These two men are big-hearted geniuses of our time who allowed me to combine the essence of their methods into the Connection Practice. That freedom was the greatest gift I've ever received.

Deeper Understanding
of the Connection Practice

When I first taught the Connection Practice, I would ask people to get coherent before starting the other steps. As I gained more experience, I observed that when feelings and needs weren't acknowledged first, it could be difficult to find the willingness to get coherent. Rick, a Rasur who leads choirs in his free time, tells a story about how this works:

> While we were preparing to go onstage at a summer concert, I noticed Tim was particularly agitated. He's a doctor at a university hospital, in charge of student health programs. He was under a lot of pressure from his manager, especially about offering counseling to stressed-out students. Added to that, his son had been arrested for painting graffiti in the past and had just been caught again.
>
> I asked if he was feeling frustrated and anxious, and I guessed that he needed a little peace and ease in his life. I could see the relief on his face as he said, "Yes." I asked if I could show him a way to get to a peaceful state in 90 seconds. He looked skeptical but agreed.
>
> I proceeded to teach him the Quick Coherence technique, focusing on the heart, breathing as if from the heart, then remembering a time when he appreciated his son and just feeling that for a few moments. After about 20 seconds, we got the word to go on stage—he looked at me with astonishment and asked "How did you do that?"
>
> I said "I didn't, you did." Tim went on to become a HeartMath Resilient Educator and uses these techniques in stress reduction and suicide prevention at the university.

If Rick hadn't guessed Tim's feelings and needs *before* offering coherence, I'm doubtful that Tim would have been open to trying something just before going on stage. Although there are times when it makes sense to get coherent first, usually empathy is the most effective first step for shifting negative emotions so we can get to coherence and an insight.

Over the years, I've received wholehearted feedback about the power of combining empathy and insight. An NVC trainer, Christine King, sums up her experience of adding insight to her mastery of empathy:

> The days I spent with you and the Connection Practice program were helpful in understanding the integration between NVC and HeartMath. I've known of the HeartMath program for a long time now and I've used the emWave to get to a place of coherence.
>
> What I didn't know was the insight piece. When I attempt to make a decision in my head, I can obsess and I often don't get the answer that would best serve. Insight has opened up a whole new world to me. Thank you for giving me that missing simple and powerful piece so I can receive the benefit of combining the two.

Empathy and insight are like soul mates—truly made for each other. Without the balance they provide for each other, we're not

> Empathy and insight are like soulmates—truly made for each other.

at our best. On the one hand, we can be dangerously arrogant with our insights, thinking we have all the answers. Has anyone ever implied to you, "I'm intuitive so I know what you should do"? Or perhaps you've heard someone share an "aha" in a way that communicates he is uniquely illumined as compared to others. This kind of arrogance gives our intuition, and the insights it produces, a bad name. Insight needs empathy to keep it humble.

On the other hand, empathy needs insight to lift it up. When we identify too much with our own or another's suffering, we can move out of empathy and sink into misery. We need the objectivity of insight to help us transcend our limited views and gracefully find our way through painful issues.

The partnership of empathy and insight brings equanimity to our growth, an evenness of mind in the face of all highs and lows. Using the Connection Practice simply makes this natural partnership more conscious. If we find ourselves being critical of others or feeling superior to them, or harshly judging ourselves, we can call on our empathy to help us be more compassionate. If we find ourselves continually stuck in the same negative feeling and perception of an unmet need, we can access an insight and find a creative answer that will move us toward freedom.

The teamwork between empathy and insight makes all the difference in our mastery of human relations. The universal needs we share with every human being help us connect empathically with others. At the same time, people are at different levels of maturity and we must make choices in how we interact with them. Empathy releases us from critical judgments of others; insight helps us see people as they are and gives us the caring discernment we need to interact in the best way.

Our Inner Balance

Once we know how to access and integrate these inner partners, our natural balance emerges. The Connection Practice is not the only way to access this inner balance.

Many people experience getting to balance by using NVC or HeartMath. For me, it helps to have the skill I gained from each of them and combine them.

One individual found inner balance during a course I was teaching in Houston. It was time to demonstrate the six steps of the Connection Process, so I asked for a volunteer. Lynn, a professional mediator who also teaches NVC, stepped forward and sat down beside me. I said, "Okay, Lynn, please tell us about your issue."

A tall, quiet man, Lynn explained, "Everyone thinks I'm a nice guy, especially because I'm a mediator. The truth is I'm full of judgments toward myself and resentments toward others. I'm just pleasing everyone, putting on a front, and I've been that way all my life."

I began to guess Lynn's feelings and needs around that discomfort, "Lynn, I'm wondering if you're feeling sad because this has been going on so long and you're yearning to be authentic. Is that right?"

"Yes," he said, "that's how it is."

"And I imagine you might be feeling lonely and discouraged because you'd like to have real connection with yourself and others and some hope that it could be sustained. Is that true?"

"Yes," he answered. "The worst part is how hard I am on myself. I guess the main need is my old friend, self-acceptance, but that old friend doesn't seem to help me change."

"Lynn, shall we stop here and ask for an insight about that?"

He agreed and I led Lynn into coherence. A few minutes later, a single tear slid down his cheek and he opened his eyes. He said, "I got it; somehow I moved from self-acceptance to feeling appreciation for myself for the first time ever. All my negativity melted away. Now I know *self-appreciation* is what will help me shift my inner life."

Silence came over the room as we took in the profound nature of love that was so evident in this moment. Later Lynn wrote on his evaluation, "I am in awe of the simple beauty of the Connection Practice. It makes my use of Nonviolent Communication richer and is one of the best trainings I've experienced." I'm guessing the inner balance that Lynn discovered has made him an even better mediator.

Lynn's shift into self-appreciation kept coming back to me. Many people say you have to love yourself in order to love others. The trouble is, no one ever told me exactly how to do that. I realized a feeling of self-appreciation in my heart was the most direct path to self-love; I decided to include a coherence using self-appreciation in all our courses.

Navigating Change

As the Rasurs and I teach the Connection Practice, we find that participants' relationships are often impacted immediately. Several public school teachers have shared that their marriages turned around by the time they finished our week-long course. One participant, Carol, was about to separate from her husband and, after learning the process, went home and offered empathy to him. They connected for the first time in 10 years. They're still married today, and Carol became a small group facilitator for our courses.

While we celebrate these successes, the Connection Practice is not directed toward a specific outcome, such as couples staying together. Rather, it's a tool that helps us navigate change. Many years ago, I participated in mediation between myself and an employee, James, who had taken some inappropriate actions. I wanted to stay connected to James, but did not want to continue with him as an employee. It soon became obvious that the mediator was attached to an outcome: he wanted James to continue as an employee. This attitude got in the way and the mediation ended with us feeling more separate rather than more connected. Later, the mediator realized his error and apologized. That experience taught me not to get attached to one idea of how things should go and, instead, allow empathy and insight to be the change agents.

We pass that concept on in our courses. A Korean student at the University for Peace explains:

> After experiencing the Connection Practice in the past five days, I realized my core needs come from my distorted relationship with my father. Now I have a strong desire to resolve my lifetime conflict with him. Since I've tried so many times, but failed to better the situation, I've been scared to face another failure, so I've been avoiding him for a long time. My next step is giving empathy to my father. I won't fear this time whether I succeed or fail because connection is first, outcome is second.

Sometimes people wonder whether both individuals in a conflict must know the Connection Practice in order for it to work. It's helpful if they do but not essential, as is obvious in many examples that I've shared. To prevent or resolve a conflict, activating the powerful partnership of empathy and insight within one person will create a change and, often, that's all that's needed.

Many people feel elated after their first exposure to the Connection Practice because it offers such efficient, powerful growth. As we mature with it, we become more sensitive to anything that doesn't feel right inside. We simply can't tolerate the numbness and pain that come from being disconnected. And when life isn't working well, we slow things down so we can pay attention to what's going on and see any dysfunctional patterns we're playing out in our lives.

Healing the Trauma of Unmet Core Needs

Dysfunctional patterns are often driven by traumas we've experienced, where we perceived a need wasn't met and then we formed a belief that it would never be met. Driven by this belief, we continue perceiving this core need is not met in many situations in our lives. Or we may believe that we can only meet that need with a particular strategy that may be painful to ourselves and others. The Connection Process helps us uncover the deep wounds that we've buried and heal them so we can stop being held hostage by the past.

Almost 20 years ago, a pattern in my behavior became obvious to me. I'd been rushing to get some things done and felt very tense, when I suddenly realized this was my habitual way of being. I remarked to my husband that I felt as if a huge hand was relentlessly pushing on my back, never letting up as I moved through the deadlines of any given day.

We're all subject to stress when there are things to do and it appears there isn't enough time to do them. Now I could see that my reactions were well beyond the normal range and negatively impacted those around me. I looked back and remembered the manager at my first job saying, "Will you relax? You're making me nervous." I looked at other feedback I'd received and could see this had been going on forever; it had been a blind spot all the while.

A year later, I was in Kansas City for a visit and had lunch with my mother at a restaurant. On an impulse I asked, "Mom, could you tell me exactly what happened at my birth?"

She said, "The doctor who delivered you was also a minister. He needed to get to church for an activity at the same time I was in labor, so he was in a big hurry for you to be born. He pushed and pushed and pushed trying to get you out faster. He pushed so hard on my stomach that I turned black and blue."

As I heard these words, a wrenching sob began to rise up from my gut. I didn't want Mom to feel bad about sharing this, so I excused myself to have a good cry in the bathroom. Finally, I understood where that giant hand on my back had come from. I'd formed a belief about life from that experience: *I have to hurry up and get everything done in order to survive. That's what life wants from me.*

Realizing what had happened at my birth was helpful, but it was the Connection Practice that set me free from acting it out the rest of my life. The core need that was programmed into me at birth, and felt like it could never be met, was efficiency. When I asked for an insight about that, I heard the words: *Show yourself that you're free to be.*

I thought about ways I could act on that insight. There was a three-day certification seminar coming up at the Institute of HeartMath. I knew I would want to perform well at this seminar and do everything on time—the kind of pressure that typically triggers me. With my new insight, my goal was to move through the whole evaluation, just knowing I was free to be. If I got triggered, I planned to silently name my feelings of worry and stress, name my core need of efficiency, and move into coherence, filling up with self-appreciation and time to just be. I wouldn't need to access an insight as I already had the insight I needed. I just wanted to break the pattern.

I did it! After giving my presentation, the instructor said, "Rita Marie, what presence you have." Those words made my heart sing. I knew if I'd been frenetic as I'd been in the past, I wouldn't have had a powerful presence. Now I've almost entirely extinguished that old trigger and I give myself more time to just be. If I do get triggered, I bring back the memory of showing myself I'm "free to be" at the Institute of HeartMath and I'm empowered anew.

Core unmet needs can sabotage relationships, especially if both people are being triggered at the same time. This happened to me one evening when I attended a meeting with a longtime friend, Jane, who was also a Rasur. The meeting ended and I received a phone call on the land line there. As I began talking, Jane began jumping up and down, waving her arms vigorously and making faces to let me know she wanted to leave right away. I got triggered by this; it was like my birth experience of being pushed to do something before I was ready. I felt angry but didn't want to say something I would regret, so I didn't address it and we left shortly afterwards.

Later I sat down and completed a Connection Process worksheet on this situation. I knew that I'd reacted because of my history, but Jane had seemed charged up too. I remembered other times when she was ready to leave and communicated in similar ways. As I guessed her feelings and needs, I wondered if these situations were triggering her need to matter. The insight that followed my empathy was: *You can ask Jane and set yourselves free.*

The next time I was with Jane, I brought up the issue and guessed that, when she wants to leave and has to ride with someone, it's really important to her to matter. She recognized this pattern of her behavior and we began to explore it. She knew that, at her birth, her mother held back letting her out of the womb because she wanted her father to be at the birth. Jane had been forced to wait a long time when everything in her was ready to be born.

Suddenly Jane saw the connection between her birth and her anxiety in situations where she wants to leave. All her life, she had yearned to matter as much to her parents as they mattered to each other. As Jane discovered the cause of her reactions, my frustration with her past behavior melted into compassion.

We were in awe of this new awareness; both of us had been triggered by our birth experiences—her waving her arms and saying "Let me out of here!" and me saying "Don't push me out of here!" We knew coherence would help us further overcome those old, irrational reactions. We'd found compassion for one another and set ourselves free by walking our talk of connection.

Perceptions of core unmet needs are not limited to our birth experiences. They can come from any trauma. One of our graduates relates:

> My mother had a core need from a trauma that
> she had never resolved. As she was dying, thanks
> to the Connection Practice, I was able to give
> her empathy by guessing her feelings and needs
> around that very sensitive issue. I reached the little
> girl inside her that had been hurt from that event
> and gave her the empathy and love she'd needed
> all her life. To share this with my mother was
> surely one of the most important moments in my
> life. I will always be thankful for knowing *how* to
> hold my mother's hand through it.

Trauma from being parented is a factor in the formation of core needs for many of us. One of our graduates, Cat, shares how she is able to transform those needs now:

> I'm using the Connection Practice when I run up
> against pesky, painful memories, the ones that
> continually pop up. Now I go "back in time" and
> change how I felt when it happened.

When I was in second grade, I was struggling to learn to read. My dad decided he'd help me. He invited me to sit on his lap and read to him. I was so thrilled. My dad never let me sit on his lap or held me in anyway and this felt wonderful. I began reading and soon he slapped me on the leg, shook the book at me and screamed, "There's no 'have' in that sentence. Why are you saying 'have'—do you see it?" and on it went. I cried; he put me down and he never held me on his lap or tried to help me again.

As a little kid, I couldn't conceive of the demons that haunted my dad and, even today, I'm only guessing. He was deeply wounded and his anger was often out of control. By using the Connection Practice, I've changed the focus of that incident from my hurt to empathy for his hurt and pain. My insight was that, in the end, it wasn't about me. It was about his inability to help me, or himself, in a constructive way.

My point is that the Connection Practice can change what might be called a "negative defining moment" to an "enlightened moment."

Inner healings like these are precious turning points. We can stop being held hostage to the past and live fully again, once we know how.

A Science Summary

Years after creating the Connection Practice, I came to understand the scientific basis for the compatibility between empathy and insight. I mentioned each of the studies when

I explained the aspects of the practice earlier in these pages. When we put them all together, we can get a more complete picture of why the Connection Practice works:

1. *Naming Feelings Reduces the Reaction of the Amygdala:* In *Putting Feelings into Words*, researchers found that naming feelings reduced the amygdala's response.[30] Naming feelings is the first step in the Connection Practice.

2. *Naming Needs Leads to Empathy:* In the *Neural Substrate of Human Empathy: Effects of Perspective-taking and Cognitive Appraisal* study, behavioral measures and brain responses showed that when subjects had a context for understanding another person's needs, it enhanced their empathic responses.[31] Naming needs is the second step in the Connection Practice.

3. *Heart-Brain Coherence Leads to Insights:* A *Brain Mechanism for Facilitation of Insight by Positive Affect* [32] reported that people in a better mood are more likely to solve problems by insight. Heart-brain coherence changes an individual's mood to one of positive affect, which results in the insights that are tapped in the last step of the Connection Practice.

We know from the evaluations of over 2,000 people from all walks of life that the steps of the practice reduce their irrational reactions and give them greater access to insight for daily living. I have touched lightly on scientific research because my emphasis is on applying what we know and experiencing its impact. To enrich our understanding of why it works, there's an abundance of research on feelings, empathy, compassion, coherence and insight, some of which is listed in the Resources Section on page 241.

Connecting the Dots of the Connection Practice

No matter what is happening in life, the steps of the Connection Practice get you completely connected. By connecting in five ways, you become more aware and masterful in responding intelligently.

After you identify your situation, you:

1. Connect your feelings to a met or unmet need.
2. Connect to another person's feelings and needs through respectful guessing (if someone else is involved).
3. Connect to heart-brain coherence through positive feelings.
4. Connect to your best intelligence and access an insight.
5. Connect your inner life to your outer life by acting on the new awareness you have gained.

The Rasurs and I now teach the Connection Practice to businesses, universities, government, schools, nonprofits and the general public. It efficiently and substantially transforms our lives into happier places to be, yet to embody it takes commitment and practice. Ralph Ellison, American novelist, said, "It takes a deep commitment to change and an even deeper commitment to grow." Imagine the rich rewards of consciously creating connection for the rest of your life.

Chapter Summary

1. The Connection Process, the first part of the Connection Practice, is the core activity.
2. The second part, the Connection Path, helps resolve all manner of conflicts and heal issues.
3. The third part, the Connection Mediation, is an intervention between two people in a conflict with the help of a mediator.
4. Guessing others' feelings and needs reduces the emotional charge so that others become more willing to get coherent.
5. Getting attached to an outcome creates a barrier to connection.
6. The Connection Practice can heal lifelong core issues.

5.

Using the Connection Practice to Overcome Challenges

Connection as a Life Preserver

I hung on to the Connection Practice when my life took a radical turn from 2009 to 2012. Here's what happened:

- February 2009—The economic downturn resulted in losing the funding for the Costa Rican program that had taken us into 24 schools. I had to lay everyone off but the director. I wasn't sufficiently adept at the Connection Practice to handle this well, and the employees left in a huff.

- July 2009—My husband, a minister, told me he'd been having a three-year affair with a woman in the church and he wanted a divorce. I was shocked at the thought of ending our 20-year relationship, which had brought me happiness and stability. (He has agreed for me to share about him in this chapter so it can help others who face similar challenges.)

- February 2010—Our divorce was final. Without adequate funding, I had to put the Costa Rican program on pause indefinitely. To remove myself from the gossip in our ruptured community and to raise funds, I began offering courses throughout the United States.

- August 2010—I moved to Arlington, Texas, to live with my father and experienced reverse culture shock; after seventeen years in Costa Rica, I was a bit lost. In just eighteen months, I had lost my marriage, my spiritual community, the work I loved in Costa Rica and my home there.
- February 2012—I was diagnosed with non-Hodgkin's lymphoma. As a result of my illness and the challenging economy, Rasur Foundation International lost its financial cushion.

Until 2009, my life had been relatively pain free. These unfamiliar extremes of adversity gave me the opportunity to test the mettle of my practice. Many times I succeeded in applying what I know; at other times I was too overwhelmed. The bottom line is that it all added up to the greatest learning in my life and solidified my daily use of the Connection Process.

Highlights of My Difficult Journey

The loss of funding for our Costa Rican program sent me into a panic; I began drinking too much Diet Coke® and eating unhealthily, unconsciously striving to find the energy to keep going. Of course, these behaviors sabotaged my coherence and I made managerial mistakes. I finally stopped to check my feelings and needs; I was worried and confused and needed clarity, stability and support. When I asked for an insight, the words came: *What you are doing has a cost.* This got my attention because it didn't have the same tone as the "shoulds" that were spinning around in my head.

Then I wanted to know exactly what to do differently, so I went back into coherence and asked for another insight. It was simply, *Use your time consciously.* After that, I got off the Diet Coke; ending that addiction helped me calm down and focus. The problem is, I'd always relied heavily on my ability to get things done faster when under stress and I returned to that old strategy rather than doing a daily Connection Process. It didn't work—it seems I couldn't see the forest for the trees—and I kept going in circles.

The news of my husband's affair turned my economic nosedive into an emotional tailspin, which forced me to dive into my practice so I could keep my sanity. I'd taught my husband the practice, so I asked him to walk the Connection Path with me in the hope we could find peace with each other. As we did that, our main needs emerged—his was acceptance and mine was shared reality. Having a shared reality means having common values and a shared belief system. My insight came: *You thought you had a shared reality with him but you didn't. Be grateful for what you did have.* That was a bitter pill to swallow, but I knew it was true, and it was the closest thing to acceptance I could offer my husband.

Walking the Connection Path took me closer to peace, but I couldn't find any meaning in this life change and I was still hurting. One night I got coherent and asked for a dream that would set me free. This is what I dreamed:

> I was down on my knees at the altar of a church. To my left was my husband and, to his left, his lover. The congregation was in back of us and a minister was in front of us. The minister said, "What a wonderful job the three of you have done in playing out this drama so that Rita Marie could learn from it and become a better teacher." At that,

I raised my hands high with thumbs up so that the
congregation could see my wholehearted agreement with that statement.

When I woke up, I had a firm grasp on the meaning of
this crisis in my life. I didn't see myself as a victim now.
Something deep inside me had brought this lesson forth and
now I was ready to learn from it. The worst of my emotional
pain was gone, but the huge ripples of change in my life
caused constant stress.

After moving to Texas, my work expanded in the United
States and I was continually up and down in airplanes,
regularly putting my body through different time zones and
environments. Suddenly, I was allergic to everything and
wasn't able to breathe well. Finally, I was diagnosed with
non-Hodgkin's lymphoma.

I processed my feelings and needs around this diagnosis.
I felt scared, but also determined to heal myself. According
to a study in *Nature Reviews Clinical Oncology*, "Traumatic
shocks, which are totally unexpected, cause a mind, brain
and body reaction that can trigger the formation of cancer."[33]

My body had been through both emotional shock and
physical stress. I felt confident I could turn that around.
When I asked for an insight, the words came: *Accept the gift
of healing*. I heard it as an affirmation that I would heal.

My oncologist, Dr. Michael Savin at Texas Oncology,
told me chemotherapy could cure this cancer quite easily.
When I explained that I wanted to try alternative methods,
he looked me in the eye, took my hands in his and said,
"It sounds like you need autonomy and that's the way it
should be." My heart opened to this gentle doctor who
knew how to give me empathy.

I began my healing journey, sorting out advice on the

internet, cleansing my body of toxins, exercising and eating the foods that help us thrive. I searched my heart for anything I'd done that had caused hurt to anyone, or anyone that had caused hurt to me, and did my Connection Process around these memories. If the process pointed toward making amends, that's what I did. Other times, I got the messages, "wait" or "this isn't yours to own," so I simply sent appreciation to whoever was involved. Whenever I asked about the cancer, I kept getting: *Accept the gift of healing.*

I was worried about the downward spiral of Rasur Foundation International's finances and my inability to attend to this while healing from cancer. I named my needs as "support" and "hope." Then the insight came: *Stand in the glory of the gift you have to give.* I took that to mean that embodying what I teach would bring the funds. Shortly after that, I had conversations with several of our supporters; they gave significant amounts and we rebounded.

A friend gifted me with a trip to Brazil to see a famous healer. I stayed in a tiny room in a hotel near the main house where the healing takes place. I was continually miserable, as the lymphoma had caused the left side of my sinuses to be blocked for almost a year. I wanted to breathe normally, but I'd tried many remedies without success.

I was lying on the tiny bed in my cozy space, gazing up at the wooden ceiling, when it dawned on me that I hadn't used the Connection Process on this physical challenge, only on the cancer in general. So I gave it a try, beginning with my feelings and needs. I felt confused, worried, uncomfortable and scared that I would never breathe normally again. I needed clarity, reassurance, well-being and freedom. Then I moved into coherence and listened for an insight.

This directive arrived: *Stand on your head.* I hadn't stood on my head for about 40 years, but I decided to try it. I placed a pillow on the floor, put my head on it, and threw my legs up against the wall. I could only handle it for a few minutes, but when I got up, I could breathe better. I tried it several more times and my nose opened up on the left side. I have continued to regularly upend myself to ensure good circulation in my sinuses.

Although I felt a sense of restoration from my time in Brazil, when I returned home, my PET scan showed I still had lymphoma. I decided to go for chemo and, after four sessions, I was in remission. I felt profoundly grateful for my inner cleansing, for the new habits I'd formed, for my health insurance, for modern and alternative medicine, and for the doctor, friends and family who helped me through it all. Every aspect was essential and it had all been a gift of healing. In hindsight, I understood why I repeatedly heard: *Accept the gift of healing.* The word "accept" had opened me to giving this healing the time and space it deserved.

Now I was ready to bounce back. I hired a new director and a training coordinator for the Costa Rican program, and they trained 860 more teachers in 2013. I forged ahead with the Rasurs in the United States, who began to teach their own Connection Practice courses and move participants along the training track toward certification.

The Most Helpful Habit

There are many approaches to personal growth, each with its own unique strength. The strength of the Connection Practice, compared to other methods, is that it takes full advantage of the power of the heart to pull the brain into a more intelligent

> The strength of the Connection Practice is that it takes full advantage of the power of the heart to pull the brain into a more intelligent state.

state. The problem with all personal growth approaches, including the Connection Practice, is in actually using them rather than just talking about them. The only way I've found to overcome that is to make my practice a daily habit.

All my life, I've resisted doing the same thing every day. Other than the basic elements of self-care, like brushing my teeth and showering, I've preferred spontaneity to discipline. I've tried writing a daily journal, but it always seems like a chore rather than a joy, so I don't follow through.

The Connection Process is a different experience altogether. Taking time each morning—sometimes five minutes, other times an hour or more—prevents me from stuffing my feelings and needs, losing touch with my best wisdom and making life worse instead of better. *Habitual disconnection requires habitual connection to undo it.*

One might think that habitually using a practice might get boring or cause us to see life in a limited way. The opposite has been true for me—the more I practice, the deeper I go and the more fascinated I become with life. I'm more trusting of myself and life now, so I'm more spontaneous. This daily habit is like a servant that has opened the door to show me into my home. Through the wisdom and compassion that dwell in my "home," I'm in touch with my essence and my freedom of choice.

It's amazing how externally focused most of us are and how much resistance we have to sitting still and going inside. My life centered primarily on my outer world because I hadn't found a consistently powerful, efficient way to manage my inner life. Even after discovering the power of the Connection Process, I found myself skipping it. I've developed seven strategies that keep me coming back to this habit, no matter what is going on in my life.

1. Using The Connection Process Daily Workbook
Our editor, Diane Blomgren, and I developed this
workbook, which includes 90 Connection Process
worksheets. Having the workbook helped me ground
my practice. Because it's small, I'm able to take it with
me everywhere and I rely on it. You can try it out with a
sample worksheet on page 214.

2. Being at the same time, same place when possible
When I'm home, sitting every morning in the same chair
to complete my process has helped me be consistent. I
look forward to sinking into that chair as I know I'm going to feel empowered afterwards. When I travel, I pick
a place to do my practice as I'm unpacking and I put my
workbook there. This visual symbol reminds me of the
uplift I get whenever I journey to my inner world.

3. Talking out loud when alone in your practice
The participants in our courses learn the Connection
Process with a partner and find that the results escalate
when someone is listening and supporting us at each
step. The students often continue working with their
partners after the course ends.

I yearned to benefit from that human connection every
day, but it wasn't realistic for me. Then I thought about
Tom Hanks in the movie *Cast Away*; stranded on an
island, he turned a volleyball into his friend, Wilson.
The connection to something outside himself helped
him survive. That awareness made me think about a
picture that hangs in my bedroom of someone precious
to me. I took the picture off the wall and began to talk
to it as I did my practice; my sessions grew even richer.

One of the Rasurs uses a candle flame in the same way. All that matters is finding a way to feel maximally connected.

4. *Talking with a Connection Partner*
   When I'm having a hard time working through an issue, I'll call on one of my friends who knows the Connection Process. That human touch usually does the trick. One day a childhood issue that I thought was put to rest came alive again. I wanted to expand the reach of our Rasur Foundation International mission and knew it would take a new level of confidence on my part. Something was holding me back—a place in my heart that still held onto some of my mother's beliefs. I took time to reflect on the events that had led up to this day:

   My mother was a get-things-done kind of person, and I'm grateful she taught me to move into action if I wanted something to happen. At the same time, my birth trauma was reinforced by her constant push to get things done (or else!).

   In several pictures of me as a child, sitting on Mom's lap, I have my right hand almost completely in my mouth, already full of anxiety and unable to enjoy the moment. As a teenager, I tried to rid myself of this anxiety by screaming at the top of my lungs, "Mom, life is not just getting things done!"

   Mom had looked blankly at me and said, "Then what is it?"

   I said, "I don't know but I'm going to find out."

   Despite that noble intention, I repressed those feelings, and my anxiety later turned into compulsive eating, lack of connection in relationships and, consequently, lack of discernment about people. Once I began using the Connection Process, my life started shifting.

On this particular morning, I realized I'd never fully released the sense of limitation I'd inherited from my mom. I had plenty of compassion for my mother, who died in 2005. She'd been through many trials in her life, and I saw her as an incredible overcomer. At the same time, she'd put a stop to my performance of funny monologues, which I'd done from the age of six, because she didn't want me to get "too big for my britches." Instead, our daily focus was on to-do lists. As an adult, I returned to some public speaking, but it was limited because I spent too much time on the humdrum of life. Now I had to completely let go of those beliefs if I was going to fulfill my purpose.

Ready to be healed at depth, I invited Daneen, my housemate and a practitioner of connection, to join me. I asked her to play "Mom" as if my mom knew exactly how to give me empathy, reflecting back my feelings and needs. Daneen quietly listened to me pour out the pain of my childhood and responded, "When I put a stop to your performing and constantly pushed you to get things done, it seems you felt hurt and angry because you needed understanding and support. I'm guessing you were also sad and lonely because you needed to express yourself and be seen for who you are. Is that how it was?"

"Yes," I whispered and my tears of release verified

that the empathy had landed. After my session with Daneen, I moved into coherence and the insight came, *Mom is so proud of you.* That brought more tears and a profound knowing that I was free of the limitations of the past.

I had processed my relationship with my mother before, but Daneen's caring presence as a Connection partner helped me heal at a much deeper level. Now I can imagine that Mom wants me to share about our relationship so others can learn how to free themselves from generational pain. Daneen helped me get to this point. Friendships like ours, based on mutual empathy, honesty and trust in each other's insights, are worth gold.

Relationships that have the Connection Practice as a mutual framework are invaluable when we're in such emotional or physical pain that we're unable to do the practice. When I was going through chemo, I stayed with my sister, Shari. At times, the nausea and brain fog were so intense that I couldn't keep up my daily practice.

One day, while in that zombie state, I needed to make an important decision about my treatment plan. My thoughts and feelings were swirling in circles and Shari stepped in. She's a Rasur so she didn't try to tell me what to do, and she didn't console or sympathize. Instead, she listened and then guessed my feelings and needs. This level of empathy—of feeling truly heard— got me through the fog to the insight I needed for that next step.

5. *Stimulating positive feelings with music and physical activity*

Occasionally, I can't find the will to do my practice.
In those times, I dance alone to golden oldies, which
quickly sends me into coherence. As feelings, needs and
insights come up while I dance, I pause and jot them
down. Before long, my mood has lifted and I'm ready
to jump back into life. For other people, it might be
singing or walking or doing something creative. When
we know what activity efficiently brings us back into a
positive feeling state, we can use it to help us face what's
going on inside.

I had the opportunity to meet Meaghan Kennedy
Townsend, granddaughter of Robert Kennedy and a
top-notch yoga instructor. Meaghan was initiating a
new program for schools and wanted to learn about the
Connection Practice. As I educated her about the steps of
the practice, she educated me about how to use posi-
tions of the body to shift specific negative emotions into
positive ones. I was wowed. Although I use short physical exercises in seminars to shift the energy and change
the mood, I hadn't realized how the body is an actual
support to social-emotional learning. Now I see being
connected to our bodies is essential to being "completely
connected."

6. *Focusing on celebrations as well as challenges*

I was resistant to focusing on a challenge every day
as it focused my attention solely on problems. When
we changed the workbook to include processing cele-
brations, that resistance melted away. Here is a happy
moment from one of my worksheets:

Celebration:

Today I realized that an insight I had a year ago has proven true. I'd been distressed about seeing a beautiful property that I once owned deteriorate under the new owners. When I had processed that pain, the insight that came was: *You're going to higher ground.* This helped me detach from the appearance of the grounds. Now this situation has evolved and I can see I'm truly arriving at higher ground.

My feelings: Awestruck, grateful, trusting, hopeful

My needs: My met needs are clarity, meaning, purpose and transcendence

Insight: Celebrate yourself for playing your part in turning this into something good.

How I will act on my insight: It's easy to be grateful when a situation turns out well, but I usually forget to give myself any appreciation for it. When things turn out well from now on, I'll remember to celebrate my role in them.

7. *Attending a Connection Practice Group*
   We can grow from participating in Practice Groups, too. In all of our courses and groups, the sharing is confidential. We also make this agreement: *We don't talk about another person who is known by the group when they're not present. If you want to bring up an issue with a person in the group, first ask in private if the other person is willing. It is okay for the person who is asked to say "no."* As a result of this agreement, we create emotional safety in our activities, and people feel free to open up.

Growing Reliably and Gracefully

Practicing connection each day is a bit like drinking water. We may think we don't need much water, but we can easily become dehydrated and not know what hit us. Consequently, experts advise us to be proactive in drinking water.

Likewise, we may think we don't need to practice being connected as we're feeling fine and handling whatever comes our way. When issues come up, though, we need a reserve of skill at our disposal. If we've practiced every morning, and throughout the day as needed, we are well-prepared for the stresses of life. As Doc Childre, HeartMath founder, says, "A little practice is a small price to pay for accessing the connection to the caretaker within."[34]

> If we've practiced every morning, and throughout the day as needed, we are well-prepared for the stresses of life.

Over time, the Connection Process builds solid self-worth based on an internal locus of control. You become indispensable to yourself, yet you also become a better listener and are more aware of other people's needs. I found that it improved my social life, as I used to be a bit shy at parties. Now, before attending a party, I set an intention to treat each person there to a healthy helping of empathy. The results are exhilarating—I breeze past small talk and get to see the light in each person's eyes as they feel heard, whether they share something positive or negative. My attitude has shifted completely—bring those parties on!

The more you practice, the more you realize you may not be able to choose what happens to you, but you can always choose what happens *through* you. No one can take away your powers of empathy and insight; you're as solid as a rock. You're not at the mercy of others or circumstances, and you're joyfully propelled toward fulfilling your deepest desires.

On the other hand, there will be times when the connection you want with another person doesn't materialize or the conflict doesn't get resolved. We can't control what others choose to do—our attachment to a particular response from them just gets in the way. In those disappointing moments, we give ourselves empathy, and we can always silently send the other person empathy.

I experienced that situation with my ex-husband. He has courageously agreed for me to share the truth of it here, as he's striving to be authentic and heal his life. After we parted ways, he eventually resigned from the church and moved back to the United States. After his departure, unethical actions he had taken in the church came to light. For the second time, the consequences of his behavior to the church were debilitating.

I spent 16 years of my life supporting this church with my heart, hands and finances; now it had few members left and no funds to hire a new minister. I didn't want to give up on it and wished he would make amends to all those who'd left the church and the few who still hung on. That course of action could help the church make a clean start. I took this issue to my Connection Process to see what might come out.

As I contemplated my ex-husband's behavior and all that I knew of his past, it wasn't hard to open my heart to his needs. He was trying to find his way out of an inauthentic life, but confusion around how to do that had caused his strategies to backfire. I guessed he was feeling scared and hurt and yearned for acceptance, peace, authenticity, autonomy and ease. I wanted to support his needs being met and also wanted to see the needs of the church met.

I communicated with him, giving him empathy, then sharing my honesty and my request to help the church heal. I was distressed to find that he wasn't willing to make amends. I knew I had to let that go; otherwise, it was actually a demand, not a request. I was satisfied I'd done the best I could to be empathic and honest, but I was still painfully disappointed in him, in the prospects for the church, and in life. I processed my feelings and needs and found my main need was hope. I listened inside, but no insights arrived that set me free of a profound sense of loss; a huge part of my heart had shut down—the part that had loved and believed in him completely.

Finally, one day an insight showed up: *To love everyone, you must love every one.* I saw that I wouldn't love life wholeheartedly until I let myself love my ex-husband wholeheartedly again. Now each day, I silently send him the same love I had for him for 20 years. I'm free to love all of life once again. I doubt I would have found peace around this unresolved conflict without the help of my practice. The dream I'd had about being at the altar with my husband and his lover had forecast this lesson; having learned how to heal deep emotional pain, I could now teach from a more authentic place. I have been able to move on, and my ex-husband has shared with me about his new start in life. I wish him well on his journey.

People learn the Connection Process at their own speed, and I've never known any participants who didn't make progress. But it's not a magic wand that you can wave once and fix all your behaviors. Like the well-known 12-Step Program, "It works if you work it." It's much easier to stay in our comfort zones; what is automatic in our responses is also securely familiar. Like many things of value in life, connecting inside and out requires commitment and practice, practice, practice.

I'm thankful that the rewards of my practice are so tangible and tantalizing; I got hooked for life. As I grew, I became calmer and more confident. However, I'm still a fallible human being. I found myself with lymphoma again in 2014. I couldn't believe it; I felt ashamed of my failure to have a healthy body as I believe that connection should result in good health. I knew that my shame was fueled by fear of other people's judgments; I imagined I would lose their respect and they would disconnect from me. That's the root fear that's at the heart of shame. So I dove deeper into my practice to release that fear and discover what was triggering lymphoma in my life.

I processed my feelings and needs; I felt deeply discouraged as I value radiant health, and I thought that not smoking, rarely drinking alcohol, eating mostly vegetarian and being vigilant about cleaning out negative emotions should be enough to achieve it. I felt concerned over the stability of our work, as pioneering in this field requires constant fundraising and that role rested primarily on my shoulders. I also felt vulnerable and wary because I wanted factual information, understanding and empathy about the cause of my lymphoma, not opinions or analysis.

When I sought an insight, a memory from 2012 came floating into my awareness:

> When I was trying to heal from lymphoma by alternative means, I was making a Connection Practice video with a professional team. They set me up in a room with several cameras and extra lighting. While we were filming, someone noticed that one of my lymph nodes seemed to be getting bigger. As we continued, the node grew before our eyes. Finally, it became so big it couldn't be hidden

from the camera. It was pressing on my throat, and
I was worried it might keep me from breathing.
We stopped filming and my friends took me to an
emergency room.

This memory promptly sparked an insight: *The electromagnetic field (EMF) that I'm exposed to every day, similar to the electricity from the cameras and the lights, is triggering the lymphoma.* Afterwards, I found evidence that workers with exposure to electric fields have elevated risks of non-Hodgkin's lymphoma and discovered other research that indicates exposure to EMFs can result in cancer.[35, 36] I have high exposure from airplanes, long hours on my laptop and cell phone, and Wi-Fi wherever I go. I began to eliminate EMFs as much as possible from my environment to strengthen my immune system.

All these experiences have taught me to shift from asking, "What's wrong with me?" to "What's going on with me?" Then, using the Connection Process, I approach myself with curiosity and acceptance.

> Shift from asking, "What's wrong with me?"
> to "What's going on with me?"

Many other people have joined me in this method of personal evolution. My friend Sam has been practicing connection since he took my course in 2008. He shares:

> I continue to practice because it reminds me that
> outward blaming doesn't help. My critical self-
> talk is being healed as my subconscious thoughts
> become conscious. The Connection Process
> sends me inward. Now I have the capacity for

self-empathy and for bringing my questions and answers to light.

Skills like the ones that Sam has acquired add up to emotional competence. Dr. Gabor Maté, in his book *When the Body Says No*, spells out what emotional competence requires:

- the capacity to feel our emotions so that we are aware when we are experiencing stress;
- the ability to express our emotions effectively and thereby to assert our needs and to maintain the integrity of our emotional boundaries;
- the facility to distinguish between psychological reactions that are pertinent to the present situation and those that represent residue from the past. What we want and demand from the world needs to conform to our present needs, not to unconscious, unsatisfied needs from childhood. If distinctions between past and present blur, we will perceive loss or threat of loss where none exists; and
- the awareness of those genuine needs that do require satisfaction rather than their repression for the sake of gaining the acceptance or approval of others.[37]

The emotional competence, self-knowledge and empowerment that flow from the Connection Practice can't be captured in words; however, this poem comes close. It describes a shift from endlessly seeking external sources of love to discovering love of self. Imagine achieving self-love at this level . . .

Love after Love

The time will come
when, with elation,
you will greet yourself arriving
at your own door, in your own mirror,
and each will smile at the other's welcome

and say, sit here. Eat.
You will love again the stranger who was your self.
Give wine. Give bread. Give back your heart
to itself, to the stranger who has loved you

all your life, who you ignored
for another, who knows you by heart.
Take down the love letters from the bookshelf,

the photographs, the desperate notes,
peel your own image from the mirror.
Sit. Feast on your life.

—Derek Walcott

Chapter Summary

1. Using the Connection Practice consistently redirects you from ignoring your feelings and needs and losing touch with your best wisdom.
2. Having a reservoir of skill by practicing connection regularly will prepare you for stressful moments.
3. The Connection Practice builds self-worth based on an internal locus of control.
4. You may not be able to choose what happens to you, but you can always choose what happens *through* you.
5. You can shift from "What's wrong with me?" to "What's going on with me?"

6.

Creating Connection at School and at Home

We Can Stop Generational Violence

Do you remember the story of Joe that I shared in chapter one? He'd pulled his classmate across the playground by her hair after failing a math exam. After identifying his needs and becoming coherent, Joe realized he could ask for support rather than hurting someone. Children everywhere would benefit from that same understanding; it changes the course of their lives and makes life better for all of us.

Every day, 565 young people across the world die from interpersonal violence, which is defined as violence that occurs between people who know each other.[38] What if teaching the combo of empathy and insight could dramatically decrease youth violence? I'm certain if these skills were considered as essential as reading, writing and arithmetic, and included in education systems around the world, we would see a remarkable reduction of those violence statistics.

Joe's story is just one of many that provide evidence for that assertion. A California educator, Tecla Garcia, took the

Connection Practice course and then tried it out with her students. She reported:

> I used it with one of my fifth grade students who had been disrupting the classroom and successfully seeking negative attention. At the end of the session, he asked me, "I could use this to connect with people, couldn't I?" He had discovered a positive way to get his needs met.

Encouraged by this success, Tecla tried it with Billy, a depressed eighth grader. She explained:

> I asked him if he had a need to matter. He responded, "There's no way I would matter to anybody. It's pointless to even think about because that's not how life goes." At the end of the session, I told Billy he was important to me and that I knew he mattered to his dad, his brother and his resource teacher.
>
> The next week his resource teacher spotted me in the courtyard and called out to me. He told me that Billy was doing noticeably better. His P.E. teacher also sought me out and said his behavior had turned around; now he was coming in anywhere from first to third place in running the mile.

A study by the Centers for Disease Control and Prevention in 2013 showed that about one out of six students had seriously considered attempting suicide during the last 12 months, and one out of 12 had attempted suicide.[39] In 2012, over 5,000 teens committed suicide.[40] Just consider how depression, which can lead to suicide, could be reduced through the experience of consistent connection.

Students are also at risk of dropping out of school, which leaves them isolated and with little support for moving forward in life. *The Silent Epidemic*, a study conducted for the Bill and Melinda Gates Foundation, found that lack of connection within the school environment is one of the primary reasons that students drop out.[41] When the Connection Practice is applied daily in a school, students feel heard and experience a heightened sense of belonging, the best antidote to this modern-day problem.

Violence, suicide and dropping out all have their roots in lack of connection, as shown by study after study. It's time to put connection on the top of the priority list. Children who have mastered the art of connection will grow up and have their own children and pass this gift on to them. Then the hand-me-down of generational pain and violence will be exchanged for a heritage of creative intelligence and connection.

> Children who have mastered the art of connection will grow up and have their own children and pass this gift on to them.

A study on psychosocial risk factors of students published in the *Journal of Studies on Alcohol* backs me up on that optimistic view. The researchers discovered that students who participate in social-emotional learning (SEL) programs are less likely to engage in high-risk behaviors that interfere with learning, such as violence and drug and alcohol use.[42]

Social-emotional learning is education that teaches us to effectively manage our inner lives, see the impact of our choices, enrich our relationships and maintain a positive outlook. The Collaborative for Academic, Social and Emotional Learning (CASEL[g]) is working to make SEL an integral part of education from preschool through high school. Their evidence-based approach has been moving this field forward.

In 2008, CASEL conducted three large-scale reviews of research on the impact of SEL programs on elementary and middle-school students that included 317 studies and involved 324,303 children. They concluded:

> SEL programs yielded multiple benefits in each review and were effective in both school and after-school settings, and for students with and without behavioral and emotional problems. The programs improved students' social-emotional skills, attitudes about self and others, connection to school, positive social behavior, and academic performance; they also reduced students' conduct problems and emotional distress. Comparing results from these reviews to findings obtained in reviews of interventions by other research teams suggests that SEL programs are among the most successful youth-development programs offered to school-age youth. In addition, SEL programming improved students' achievement test scores by 11 to 17 percentile points, indicating that they offer students a practical educational benefit.

CASEL concluded that "a strong commitment to the high-quality implementation of research-based SEL programming will promote the current functioning and future development of children and youth." Another advocate for SEL,

---

g. CASEL is the nation's leading organization advancing the development of academic, social and emotional competence for all students. www.casel.org

the NoVo Foundation, believes that "SEL, brought to scale, can and will play a significant role in shifting our culture of systemic inequality and violence toward a new ethos that values and prioritizes collaboration and partnership."[43]

I'm heartened by the monumental efforts of CASEL and the NoVo Foundation, who have helped make headway in achieving a commitment to SEL programs in schools. Yet all of us in this field are faced with teachers who are under pressure to teach toward passing tests. The most frequent comment that I hear from teachers is, "I don't have time for SEL in my classroom."

With this limitation, it's challenging to bring SEL programs to scale so the majority of students can be reached. But what is the cost of not resolving this issue? Dr. Maurice Elias, a leading child psychologist, researcher and expert on SEL from Rutgers University, explains the dangers of omitting social-emotional programs from our children's classrooms.

> Many of the problems in our schools are the result of social and emotional malfunction and debilitation from which too many children have suffered and continue to bear the consequences. Children in class who are beset by an array of confused or hurtful feelings cannot and will not learn effectively. In the process of civilizing and humanizing our children, the missing piece is, without doubt, social and emotional learning. Protestations that this must be outside of and separate from traditional schooling are misinformed, harmful and may doom us to continued frustration in our academic mission and the need for Herculean efforts in behavioral damage control and repair. The roster of social casualties will grow ever larger.[44]

Meeting the Need for Efficient, Scalable SEL

To move away from this dismal picture, we need the most efficient SEL program possible. The Connection Practice Curriculum was designed to meet that challenge and offers the same steps as the adult version. In just six lessons of 30 minutes each, students learn the skills of naming and guessing feelings and needs, achieving heart-brain coherence, receiving an insight and using the Connection Process. To make it fun and easy for students, we created the Connection Process Game, which they can play alone or with a partner. It's usually more beneficial for students when they do it in pairs. This game is repeated, first thing every morning, and can be played in just 10 minutes, guided by the teacher.

> We need the most efficient SEL program possible. The Connection Practice Curriculum was designed to meet that challenge.

The Connection Process Game

During the game, students are paired up; one of them shares a situation and the other is in a support role. If the first student has shared a positive situation, they use the game to celebrate it; if it's negative, they use the steps to resolve it. Whether the youngster is sharing or supporting on a given day, this daily routine ensures that each one feels connected to his peers and teacher. The game doesn't get boring because life supplies new material every day.

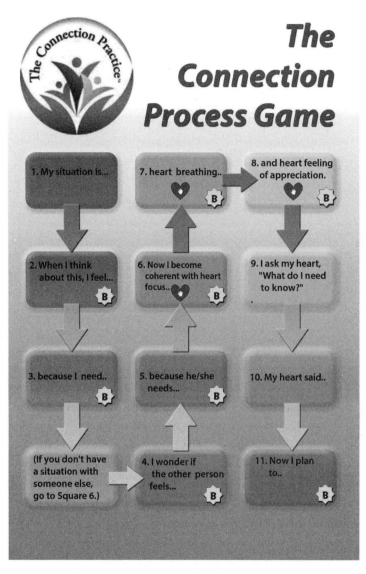

The Connection Process Game

When students play this game each morning, they feel heard and know they matter. Copyright © 2015 Rasur Foundation International. (See color illustration on page 255.)

Since only one student shares each morning, the game can be completed in 10 minutes. Those few minutes clear away emotional turmoil and excessive excitement so that each student is focused and ready to learn. As a result, the teacher spends less classroom time on managing behavior problems. Most importantly, this practice guarantees that, every day, students will know they matter; they've had the chance either to be heard or to contribute to the well-being of another.

> The practice guarantees that, every day, students will know they've had the chance either to be heard or to contribute to the well-being of another.

Here is an example of a teacher leading the game from the front of a fifth grade classroom. The students have all pushed their desks together so they're each sitting with a partner. They're using the laminated game board (8½ by 11 inches), erasable markers and their Feelings and Needs Lists. Melissa and Eric are partnered in the game.

Teacher: Okay, the person who will share a challenge or celebration today can begin.

Melissa: Yesterday I failed my math test, and then last night my dad had to sign a note from the teacher about it. He got mad and yelled at me.

Eric: *(Looking at the feelings list.)* I'm guessing you might feel hurt. Is that right?

Melissa: Yes. *(She writes this on the feelings step.)*

Eric: *(Still choosing from the feelings list.)* How about upset?

Melissa: Yes, that's true. *(She adds this feeling to the step.)*

Eric: *(Further skimming the feelings list.)* I'm wondering if you're feeling angry.

Melissa: *(Looking at her feelings list.)* No, I'm just embarrassed. I want to crawl in a hole. (She adds "embarrassed" to the step.)

Eric: Okay. *(Looking at her feelings list.)* I imagine you might need some understanding. Is that true?

Melissa: Yes. *(She writes it on the needs step.)*

Eric: What about emotional safety?

Melissa: Definitely. *(She adds it to the step.)*

Eric: *(Searching for further needs on the list.)* Do you need support?

Melissa: That's for sure. I just don't know how to do better in math.

Eric: Okay, let's guess what your dad's feeling.

Melissa: He was mad. *(She writes this on the feelings step that is for the other person.)*

Eric: *(Searching the feelings list again.)* Do you think he's worried about you?

Melissa: Yes. *(She adds it to the feelings step for the other person and looks again at the feelings list.)* And I think he's stressed about his job too. *(She adds "stressed" to the step.)*

Eric: Let's guess his needs. *(Pauses to search for a need.)* What about your well-being?

Melissa: Yes, he cares about everything that happens to me. He gets so upset though. *(She looks at the needs list.)* I think he needs peace. *(She writes "well-being" and "peace" on the needs step that is for the other person.)*

Eric: Maybe he needs clarity on how to help you do better in math.

Melissa: That sounds right. He's probably confused about that. *(She adds "clarity" to the needs step that is for the other person.)*

Teacher: Now that everyone has finished the feelings and needs steps, let's use the Quick Coherence technique to help access an insight. After you get to that happy, peaceful place inside, ask "What do I need to know about this situation?" and listen. When you get your answer, open your eyes and write it down. After everyone has their eyes open, you can share your insight with your partner.

Let's begin by focusing on our hearts. You can put your hand on your heart if it helps you focus. Down, down we go into the heart, focusing all our attention there. (She pauses to give the class time to achieve this step.)

Now let's breathe as if breathing through the heart, deeply and rhythmically. Breathe up from the belly and through the heart. (She models this by taking several breaths.)

All right, now feel appreciation down in your heart for whatever is easy for you. (She waits silently and watches as the children open their eyes.)

It looks like everyone has their eyes open, so you can share your insights with your partners now. Be sure to share how you will act on your insight, too.

Melissa: I just remembered the first time I got confused and failed a math test. After that, I just kept getting more confused. I need to go back and learn that stuff first. Then maybe I can figure out what we're learning now. Maybe my dad will help me because it's too hard to start over by myself.

Eric: What are you going to do about that?

Melissa: I'm going to explain it to my dad tonight and see if he will help me. Thanks, Eric.

Eric: You're welcome.

As they integrate the Connection Practice into their lives, kids learn how to keep their peers', teachers', and parents' needs on the table and also learn how to work as a team in solving problems.

The Connection Practice Curriculum

Here are the six lessons in the curriculum that lead up to the Connection Process Game as a daily routine. These lessons can be adapted to any age group. Each lesson focuses on an activity and a concept, which are shown below.

You will see that a lesson called "Empathy Circle" has been included. This activity brings the students together in small circles for more practice in listening and guessing each other's feelings and needs. With this skill strengthened, they will be ready to participate in the Connection Process Game.

The Connection Practice Curriculum comes with a kit of activity materials and includes emWave software, so

Activity	Concept
1. Feelings and Needs Cards	My feelings tell me about my needs.
2. Quick Coherence Technique	I know how to connect with the safe, happy place in my heart.
3. Heart-Brain Insight	I know how to listen inside for answers.
4. The Connection Process Worksheet	I can use the Connection Process to celebrate life and to solve problems.
5. Empathy Circle	I feel understood when someone guesses my feelings and needs.
6. The Connection Process Game	My buddy and I can use the Connection Process to support each other.

the children can practice coherence on a laptop set up in the classroom. Activity material templates are provided so teachers can produce the materials for more than one classroom. The kit also includes a CD of delightful songs that correspond to each lesson.[h]

Teachers who have taken Part 1 of the Connection Practice Foundations Course can purchase the curriculum. The kit is available for purchase by a school only when it's coupled with teacher training on how to implement it, as this skill is best learned through experience.

The Connection Practice In-Service Training and the Curriculum Kit give educators what they need to establish

---

h. You can find this CD under *BePeace in Song* on the page rasurinternational .org/store.

a daily foundation of SEL in the classroom. After-school programs are also ideal for immersing the students in the method, as they can practice at the beginning of each after-school session. Two Rasurs, Jan and Heidi, introduced the Connection Practice at the Community Link after-school program at Burke Elementary in Hickman Mills, Missouri. As a result of their after-school success, Jan and Heidi were able to extend the program to students during school hours and to present in-service training to the teachers.

There are other SEL components beyond what is offered in the Connection Practice curriculum. However, its efficiency allows children and youth to quickly gain the skill of connection for life, a formula for balance, focus and healthy self-esteem. Remember the story of Gabriel in chapter two, who stopped acting out once he got enough sleep? He not only solved his problem efficiently, but he started down the road of self-esteem based on an internal locus of control rather than outer rewards.

> Children and youth quickly gain the skill of connection for life, a formula for balance, focus and healthy self-esteem.

Many students in the program have reported that they used the Connection Practice at home to resolve conflicts, to the great surprise of their parents. Jan, from the after-school program mentioned above, shared, "One of our first joys was when a fourth grade girl told us she'd taught coherence to her mom and aunt one evening in their kitchen." If students around the world were able to teach their parents how to connect, what a different world we would see.

Support Teachers to Offer the Connection Practice

For children to pass the Connection Practice on to their parents or to their own children someday, we must heartily support teachers to offer it in their classrooms. Just because teachers are pressed for time in the classroom, making it difficult to add SEL, doesn't mean they don't value it. *The Missing Piece, A National Teacher Survey on How Social and Emotional Learning Can Empower Children and Transform Schools* reported that teacher endorsement of SEL holds true across education levels and school types. Nearly all teachers (95%) believe social and emotional skills are teachable and 97% think that SEL will benefit students from all backgrounds, rich or poor.[45]

The realistic approach of the Connection Practice has been consistently embraced by educators. Many educators have high social-emotional intelligence, but whether they do or not, the Connection Practice gives them a clear way to increase it and pass it on to their students. A teacher in California put it this way, "It gets to my truth quickly and helps me connect with others. I'm finally learning how to be emotionally intelligent, something I've struggled with my entire life."

By passing this learning on in their classrooms, the adults create a high degree of emotional safety and stimulate their students to have aha moments. The students also learn how to change behaviors that aren't serving them, such as bullying and misconduct.

Linda, a teacher who took the first course I offered in the United States, wrote me a few weeks afterwards:

> I've been offering empathy in my classroom and
> I'm astounded at the results, especially since I'm
> such a newbie at it. I even used it to step right in

the middle of an about-to-break-into-a-fist-fight scenario with two eighth graders this morning. I'm still smiling at the peaceful way it was resolved. The Connection Practice works!

Linda went on to become a Rasur. When teachers and administrators consistently build the social-emotional intelligence of their students, their jobs become more fulfilling and enjoyable.

Guidance counselors can utilize the Connection Practice in counseling students and parents. One guidance counselor in Texas, after learning the practice, immediately began using it as the primary tool in her interactions at the elementary school. She found the feelings and needs cards were highly effective whenever there was a conflict with students or parents, and she used the lists if it wasn't possible to lay out the cards. She was also amazed at the insights that the children shared. Each time the practice aided her in resolving situations, she would share this success with the principal. Before long, everyone was aware of the difference the Connection Practice was making in the school.

When teachers, guidance counselors and administrators have learned how to interact with their students at this level, the many rewards of a healthy social-emotional environment will motivate them to continue in this direction. As a result, more of these young people will make mature choices rather than resorting to violence. Ruth, a teacher at the José Volio School in Costa Rica, put it this way:

> I remember that Albert Einstein said insanity is continuing to do the same things but expecting different results. We can't keep doing the same things with our students and expect different results. I want them to be successful, not just academically,

but also to possess emotional intelligence. Sometimes we want to change but don't know how to do it. The Connection Practice shows us how.

> Sometimes we want to change but don't know how. The Connection Practice shows us how.

Evaluations Show Success in Costa Rica

We've been teaching the Connection Practice to school teachers, counselors, parents and children since 2004. My heart's desire is to see it offered in classrooms throughout the world. To make that possible, we've attempted to measure the impact of the Connection Practice. How do you measure subtle shifts into positive emotions and clear thinking that result in better choices? How do you measure the full impact of preventing an irrational choice? We found it easy to collect anecdotal evidence, but we also went about collecting the best quantitative evidence we could with our limited resources.

In 2004, the first Connection Practice program was implemented at the Elías Jiménez Castro School in Costa Rica. At the end of the year, 94% of the teachers reported an improvement in the quality of their communication with the students.[i]

By 2005, we had recruited a graduate student from the University for Peace and a doctoral program student from the University of Barcelona in Spain to evaluate the program at the same school. We were elated at their year-end conclusions, shown in the graph below, which compares the results from teacher surveys issued at the beginning and the end of

i. The school year in Costa Rica begins in February and ends in November.

2005. Teachers were asked how much they agreed with these statements:

1. I feel peaceful.
2. I manage my anger internally rather than acting it out.
3. I resolve conflicts creatively.
4. I identify my feelings during conflicts.
5. I express my feelings during conflicts.
6. I can identify my own needs.
7. I identify my needs during conflicts.
8. I express my needs during conflicts.
9. I make requests to get my needs met.
10. I can identify the feelings of others.
11. I help others identify their feelings.
12. I can identify the needs of others.
13. I help others identify their needs.
14. I help others to make requests to meet their needs.
15. I use nonviolent methods in my classroom.

Each choice was given a value as indicated below.

1	2	3	4	5
Never	Rarely	Sometimes	Frequently	Always

All values for each of the 15 questions were added to give each question a total value. The highest possible score for a question was 145 (or 29 teachers times 5 points if everyone answered "always").

Then these values were graphed. It was thrilling to see how much the teachers had improved markedly in every skill.

We wanted to measure the impact of the Connection Practice on students as well, but found this challenging to achieve in public schools in Costa Rica. In 2006, upon the request of our donor, the Association of Businesses for Development

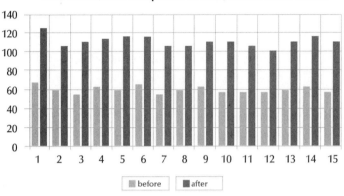

2005 Before/After Comparison at Elías Jiménez Castro School

(AED), we left our first school in order to focus on one in a troubled neighborhood.

One of our volunteers was doubtful about whether the Connection Practice would continue to have an impact after we left the Elías Jiménez Castro School. On her own initiative, she conducted teacher interviews there a year later. She was surprised at her findings. Teachers reported these lasting benefits in school:

- Aggression and violence were reduced.
- Intolerance declined and conflicts decreased.
- Students resolved conflicts by themselves.
- The Connection Practice had impacted the entire school.

They also reported lasting benefits in their personal lives:
- improvement in their self-esteem
- better communication with others
- greater empathy for self and others

Outside evaluators continued to assess our Costa Rican program each year. One unpublished study showed that misconduct reports were cut almost in half. Another indicated that relationships among teachers and with the principal improved significantly. Each time we introduce it in a school, we discover new ways that it contributes to a healthy social and emotional environment.

Impact on the Educator

One day we realized the teachers who were arriving at our headquarters for a week-long course felt resentful. Evidently they were being pressured to attend by the school directors. We gave them empathy and told them that they could either leave or stay; they stayed. On the last day of the course, one teacher said, "I didn't want to come here. Now I never want to leave."

Below is another chart of teacher response to learning the Connection Practice. In the 2008 school year, 195 elementary school teachers took our 40-hour course and completed official evaluations for the Ministry of Education. These evaluations are required for continuing education units that result in salary increases. According to the ministry, the course had succeeded way beyond our expectations, as shown in the graph below.

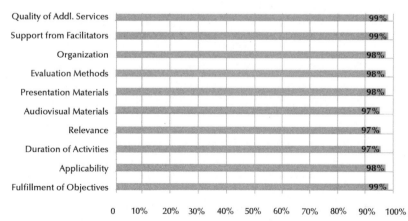

Results of 195 Evaluations for the Connection Practice Course in 2008

Category	Percentage
Quality of Addl. Services	99%
Support from Facilitators	99%
Organization	98%
Evaluation Methods	98%
Presentation Materials	98%
Audiovisual Materials	97%
Relevance	97%
Duration of Activities	97%
Applicability	98%
Fulfillment of Objectives	99%

During one of our 40-hour courses for public school teachers, a beautiful orchid went missing from our headquarters. We recognized this as an opportunity to model both empathy and honesty, so we announced the orchid was missing. Then we expressed empathy to whoever had taken it and asked if that person would be willing to return it to a spot where no one else would know.

At this, many of the teachers expressed anger and indignant judgments about the shame this person had brought on their profession. In response, I shared a story I'd heard about a tribe that handles conflict with compassion. When someone in that tribe has done something that hurts the others, they put that person in the middle of the circle and ask them to share what is going on so they can understand.

After I shared this story, the energy of the teachers shifted completely; they began to guess the feelings and needs of their colleague. Later, the person who had taken the flower returned it and expressed her profound gratitude to our trainers for the way they handled it. She talked about how her home was barren of beauty and she'd longed to change that. We gave her more empathy—and the orchid, too. She became one of the strongest advocates for the Connection Practice in her school. This was my first experience of seeing a "judgment gang" turned into a supportive community through the power of empathy.

The 1,500 Costa Rican teachers we've trained have boosted the social-emotional intelligence of the 40,000 students who were in their classrooms the year they took the Connection Practice course. Now they continue to teach it to their new classes each year, so they have reached many more. Costa Rican teacher Ivette said, "It's a privilege to be part of such an important project that will change a paradigm and, in this way, help all human beings to create a better world. I'm committed from my heart and I'm willing to continue with the program as long as needed."

Costa Rican students Douglas and Brenda model connection.
(See color photo on page 256.)

We would like to see every willing teacher in Costa Rica trained so that this country becomes a national model that can be replicated worldwide. When we achieve this, we theorize that children will thrive, dropout rates will decline, and eventually violence in the entire country will be reduced.

Schools in the United States Benefit from the Connection Practice

When I hear news reports about the United States, I often feel the pain of how polarized—and disconnected—we are in my beloved country. The rise in school shootings reflects the pain of teens who get lost finding their way through the current "fog" of constant conflict. Some people assume that my choice to live in Costa Rica was made out of rejection of my country because of its conflicts. That is simply not the case. I get choked up whenever I sing our national anthem; I'm always a bit taken aback to find such a big lump of love in my throat. I've been teaching the Connection Practice in the States since 2008 and am determined to bring the level of violence down in our schools.

By 2011, the Texas Education Agency had certified our courses for continuing education credit, and educators began to attend. In one course, I'd been particularly impressed with a guidance counselor, Lori Brady, who is also a psychotherapist. Lori's social-emotional intelligence seemed as natural as breathing. She inhaled our methodology, began using it in her interactions with the students in her elementary school, and became the champion for our first public school project. A Rasur, Judy, worked with Lori to develop a U.S.-based curriculum and test it at Oakley Elementary, a school near Houston.

After implementation, Lori shared many anecdotes about her use of the Connection Practice. Here is one:

> We had two gangs of boys in the fifth grade that were having conflicts and building toward violence. I called them together to work this out and began by leading them into coherence. Then we used the lists to put the feelings and needs of each group up on the board. Now they could see they had needs in common. The main need that emerged was communication, as one gang spoke Spanish, and the English speakers in the other gang didn't know what they were saying. Consequently, suspicion had developed between them. After forging a bond of commonality between the groups, they agreed that when they came together, they would all speak English. Soon their negative feelings had melted away and friendships were formed instead.

Lori told us about a time when the tables turned in another conflict in an unexpected way:

> A mother came to me with her daughter in tow, reporting indignantly that her daughter was being bullied by another girl. I began guessing the daughter's feelings and needs: Was she feeling scared and needing safety? Feeling lonely and needing support? After we talked about her feelings and needs, I led her into coherence and she listened for an insight. When she opened her eyes, she reported, "It's really me that has caused this—I'm the bully." It seems that the Connection Practice had opened her up so she could let go of her dishonest mask and be truthful about the situation.

Instead of criticizing and shaming bullies, it's far more transformative to teach them how to connect to themselves and others. When they build that inner competency, they no longer need to prove their competence by hurting others.

> Instead of criticizing and shaming bullies, it's far more transformative to teach them how to connect to themselves and others.

Lori related another example:

> One boy in the fifth grade suffered from extreme shyness. Every time he would try to speak up, he would turn red, freeze, and then stammer. After he learned to name his feelings and needs and achieve coherence, he was like a different person. The practice gave him access to a part of himself that set him free. He explained, "The reason I like

the Connection Practice is it just makes life easier. Whenever you're really stressed out, like I am, it helps me get through it. It's amazing how it actually works."

We created a video[46] of Lori, Judy, students, participating teachers and the principal, all talking about their experience of the Connection Practice.[j] A video production assistant, Michelle, had the opportunity to observe the children using the practice that day. She exclaimed, "What I've seen happen in the students today through the Connection Practice—the change, their confidence, their sincerity—I want to spread that around to my friends and family. I'm overjoyed about it because I've never seen this before. It's such basic ideas, but it's so sincere."

Later in the day, one student lamented, "I wish my mom and my dad knew about the Connection Practice because their jobs are very stressful. They have customers who will come in and yell at them and be mean to them." This comment reminds me of the tale of Rasur, where the children learned about connection inside their mountain school and came home each evening to share what they'd learned with their parents. What better way for connection to become a way of life?

The principal at Oakley Elementary, Penny Peacock, wrote a letter in June 2012 to sum up her experience with implementing the Connection Practice:

> As a principal, I'm always searching for new programs that will help our students be the best that they can be emotionally, socially and academically.

---

j. Taught at that time as BePeace.

I opened a new Title 1 school [a school with a large low-income student population that receives government funds] last fall, with students from four schools coming together. They all came with their own set of needs, all of which were a mystery to us. My priority was to develop a foundation that would allow for trusting relationships among students, teachers and administrators. A successful foundation would launch new possibilities of academic success, friendship and safety, and the hope for the American Dream.

. . . We started with hope, but we ended with a sense of awe and gratitude. Through the Connection Practice, teachers and students of all age levels learned how to reduce barriers and gain insight, which empowered them to bridge the gaps and make social, emotional and academic connections within our building and to the outside world. The program provided the tools, but the awe factor was in watching the students begin to own it and use it in their own lives. . . .

> The program provided the tools, but the awe factor was in watching the students begin to own it and use it in their own lives.

These many examples demonstrate that, by applying this simple practice, the rewards enrich the entire school experience—from resolving conflicts between all kinds of groups, to preventing suicide, to building self-esteem based on inner strengths rather than outer rewards. Connection is the glue. When it's missing, things fall apart. When it's present throughout a system, you have a cohesive structure that serves the needs and the learning of the human beings within it.

Summary of Connection Practice
Benefits to Students

The Connection Practice builds character in students as they learn to overcome challenges and take responsibility for their actions. Through connecting, there is a better chance that students will admit when their behavior is harmful, learn from it, and want to make amends. Consequently, it's more effective than harsh punishment.

We know from many research studies that coherence can raise academic test scores by 10 to 25 points, so that in itself is reason to rely on the Connection Practice in the classroom. As the students learn to access their best intelligence, their quality of life is holistically impacted and they become braver and stronger.

To summarize, the Connection Practice gets to the root cause of social-emotional deficits in our school environments as it:

- builds self-esteem based on an internal locus of control
- creates focus and ease in learning
- opens creativity and intuition for self-expression and problem solving
- prevents bullying and reduces misconduct
- provides highly efficient conflict resolution
- boosts test scores
- facilitates teamwork between staff, teachers and counselors
- empowers students who need extra support
- provides relief to those in emotional distress
- efficiently takes SEL to scale in the school, impacting the entire environment

We want to support millions of children and youth in connecting inside and out. Our goal is to provide a scholarship for any willing teacher or parent who needs this support in order to learn the practice. Donations, grants, and a portion of the funds from our business courses help us create and sustain these programs.

> Our goal is to provide a scholarship for any willing teacher or parent who needs this support in order to learn the practice.

Taking the Connection Process into the Home

In Costa Rica, we regularly offered parent training in the schools where we worked. The Diamond Community School in Florida, a school that I mentioned in chapter three, is implementing the Connection Practice with parents, too. Their founder, Dr. Doreatha Fields, reported:

> Diamond had an AWESOME parent meeting tonight! Karen and I shared why we chose this curriculum for our school. Then the teachers shared their success stories with the students, explained the kit contents and told how they're implementing it in the school. The parents were excited to learn how this practice had benefitted their children.
>
> The GREAT NEWS is that when we asked the parents if they would be interested in participating in the Connection Practice training, there was an overwhelmingly, enthusiastic "YESSS!"

Once parents learn the practice, they can immediately apply it at home. One parent, Kaja, explains how it has made a difference in her family:

> My daughter, Stella, is seven years old. One day when she came home from school, I saw she was sad. I asked, "Stella, would you help me practice the feelings and needs cards?" She was willing, so I put the cards out in front of her and asked, "What's up?"
>
> She said, "Lina won't let me play with her and Erica at recess. They just run away when I come up to them." This had been going on for two months, and I knew Stella was very hurt by it.
>
> "Okay, I'll make some guesses about how you feel about this. Do you feel sad? Hurt? Lonely?" She picked up the cards that reflected her feelings. Then we went over to the needs cards. I made some guesses of her needs—to matter, to be heard, acceptance, and then I guessed support.
>
> She jumped up from her chair saying "YES, YES, YES! That's what it is. I need support." She took the card from me and put it to her heart and then kissed it!!! I was amazed to see how liberated she was by naming that need. I asked her where she could get support at school and she named a boy she played with and a teacher.
>
> After this, Stella and I had a new way to communicate. The whining and angry outbursts stopped. In the morning, I ask her what support she needs for her day to go well and, at the end of the day, we

explore her feelings and needs about how it went. I'm so thankful for this breakthrough.

A couple of weeks later, Lina's mother told me their family was packing to move back to Japan. She wondered if Lina could come to our house and play the whole day so the parents could focus on the job at hand. I talked to Stella about it and she was very hesitant; she was scared that it wouldn't go well. I encouraged her to try connecting, especially since Lina was leaving for Japan and this would be the last opportunity to work it out.

Stella was nervous and acting out in the days leading up to the playdate. I guessed her feelings and needs and asked if she wanted to bring the issue up with Lina. She wanted me to do it.

After Lina arrived, I had the girls come into the kitchen and help make pancakes. As we cooked, I asked some questions about recess and recalled how scared I felt as a kid when I didn't have anyone to play with. When Stella went to the bathroom, I asked Lina if she had ever felt left out. She said she had, and I guessed how she felt and what she needed when that happened. Then I explained that Stella had felt left out during recess and was sad about it. After that, I dropped the subject. The girls had fun the rest of the day. As they said goodbye, they hugged each other.

Two days later there was a knock on the door, and there stood Lina and her mom. Lina gave Stella an envelope while her mom and I chatted for a few minutes, then off they went.

Stella opened the card and, in Lina's handwriting, it said:

Dear Stella,

Thank you for being my friend all the time. I am sorry. I might have left you out for a while and was playing with Erica only. I will never forget you even when I am in Japan.

From Lina

I was so touched by the look of wonder on Stella's face at this beautiful outcome. She started to cry, tears of release like a big sigh in her whole body. Learning to connect with herself and others will serve her the rest of her life.

Another parent, Belinda, shared how to face a typical challenge—homework.

After I learned the Connection Practice, I saw it was so simple that I'd be able to easily relay it to my 11-year-old daughter, Anabel. One evening she was struggling with organizing her homework load. She had a lot to do but kept procrastinating and just couldn't find a place to start. I asked if she would like to try something that might help her. She said yes.

I showed her the feelings and needs cards. She flipped through the feelings cards and soon found the ones that fit her situation. She felt frustrated, confused and overwhelmed. I then asked her about her needs and she sorted through the cards, finding the words ease, order and peace.

After I reflected back her feelings and needs, I asked her to remember a time when she felt positive feelings, where she had fun and there was nothing to worry about. She described going to a waterpark where she went down the big waterslides. She remembered being caught up in the moment—nothing to do, nothing to worry about—just the pleasure of the ride to the bottom and that feeling of exhilaration!

I asked her to close her eyes and listen inside for a way she could create ease, order and peace. When she opened her eyes, I asked if she wanted to tell me her insight or draw it. She drew her idea: her loft bed with a fort underneath and a table, chair, and lamp with a blanket enclosing the space. This is where she wanted to go to do her homework.

Then she quickly wrote a priority list of her homework, based on when it was due and how challenging it would be. Together we put the blanket around the space below her loft bed; she pulled her little table and a chair under there with her desk lamp. She spread out all her homework and supplies and got her list out. Then she asked me to leave but to stay close by.

I checked on her after about 20 minutes. She was steadily working on her homework and asked me to give her space. Before long she came out and said she'd finished everything that was due the next day but needed some help on her math due the day after. We made progress on the math and left the rest for the next day. Having created ease and order, she ended her day in peace with a happy heart.

A few weeks later, she described a conflict at
school and I asked her how she coped with it. She
told me she tries to be nice to the other children
and when it gets really tough, she thinks through
the feelings and needs cards and then remembers
going down the waterslides. . . .

When parents and teachers unite in using the Connection
Practice with children and youth, they create a firm foundation for actualizing the full potential of the next generation.
Mahatma Gandhi said, "Live as if you were to die tomor-
row. Learn as if you were to live forever." Imagine how the
Connection Practice will help our youngsters live and learn
to their fullest capacity as it is implemented in more schools
and homes.

Chapter Summary

1. Children who participate in social-emotional learning
   programs are less likely to engage in high-risk behaviors
   that interfere with learning.
2. A 10-minute exercise each morning can reduce behavior
   issues in the classroom and improve academic performance. At the same time, children learn they matter and
   they can contribute to the well-being of another.
3. Lack of connection is one of the primary reasons students
   drop out of school.
4. Using the Connection Process Game with students
   teaches them to have an inner locus of control that results
   in solid self-esteem.
5. Parents can use the Connection Process to help their children resolve issues.

7.

Connection in Business, Nonprofits, Government and Higher Education

Cutting the Cost of Conflict in Business and Nonprofits

An overwhelming majority (85%) of employees experience conflict at work, according to a study conducted in nine countries by the Global Human Capital Report. In the United States, the study found that employees spend 2.8 hours a week dealing with conflict, or about $359 billion in paid hours.[47]

When a business becomes proactive about conflict prevention and resolution, everyone wins. Employees feel valued, managers feel empowered, customers are treated respectfully, and the business improves its bottom line through fewer sick days, lower turnover, and more productivity from its employees.

> When a business becomes proactive about conflict prevention and resolution, everyone wins.

The Connection Practice provides a realistic, efficient way to achieve these benefits by integrating social-emotional learning every day in the workplace. The enhanced rapport and emotional safety it creates among employees results in greater commitment to the mission of the company and less resistance to change.

After learning the practice, employees are more skilled at either stopping conflicts before they start or resolving them in a manner that brings people closer. They've also learned how to consistently access their best ideas. The overall impact is that individuals are liberated to perform at higher levels of engagement, leading to a creative, cooperative culture where change is navigated with unprecedented ease. Rasurs customize the Connection Practice to the needs of each business and can include consulting, coaching, courses, and retreats.

At Rasur Foundation International (RFI), we practice what we preach: Board members, staff and Rasurs use the Connection Practice to ensure that everyone is heard. In several instances, Rasurs and employees have been disgruntled about decisions the board and I made, but we were able to walk our talk and prevent these situations from becoming hurtful conflicts.

At the same time, like all human beings, we can forget what we know, including our practice, in the heat of the moment. To reinforce our intention, we created an agreement regarding conflict resolution, which is signed by each of us. It states that we will go directly to anyone we have an issue with and use the Connection Process. If we need further support to resolve the problem, we agree to use Connection Mediation. We haven't had the need to enforce this agreement, but it serves as part of our framework for embodying what we teach.

We also use the practice to glean the best ideas from our

collective wisdom. For instance, when we wanted a new name for the practice, we asked each person in our organization to listen inside for an insight and then share their ideas. As a result, we came up with the Connection Practice, a name that simply and truly captures the essence of our work—and we made this change without resistance or conflict.

Other nonprofit organizations find that the Connection Practice works well with their missions too. In the first chapter, I mentioned Nexus, an addiction recovery center in Dallas, which is working toward training all of their staff members. The Family Place, the leading nonprofit working with domestic violence in Dallas, is also engaged in the training process. These organizations have discovered the Connection Practice is an innovative, scientifically based approach to working more effectively with both clients and staff members.

Business People Connecting
Inside and Out = Better Outcomes

Over the years, I've taught the Connection Practice to business people at their own sites and in our public courses. My first experience was in presenting a workshop for professional women within a Going to the Top seminar in Dallas with Dr. Carol Gallagher, President of the Alliance for Excellence. After just three hours, women were opening up and naming feelings and needs they'd suppressed, clearing away emotional baggage so they could make better decisions.

At times, I've been warned that the business world won't be interested in the Connection Practice, but that hasn't been my experience. Each time I've presented the basics of the practice in a business setting, the audience has been very receptive. I've spoken to businesses as diverse as Intel, the computer chip-making giant, and doctors at CIMA, the leading hospital in Costa Rica.

In the first chapter, I mentioned Anita Campion, CEO of a company that provides global consulting services to transform international development and build local capacity. A few months after her staff members took the 12-hour course, she reported back to me:

> The course helped uncover issues operating behind the scenes, which helped me better understand the motivators and stressors of the staff so I could be a better leader. One employee explained how her Asian cultural upbringing affected how she communicated. Another employee shared some stressors from home that helped me understand her feelings of vulnerability.
>
> We continue to use the Connection Practice at our Monday morning meetings, which I find helpful in getting my brain refocused after the weekend and working through challenges. One of the issues that had come up in our course was that we wanted to change the name of our company, AZMJ. Now that we knew how to access heart-brain insights, we used that process in seeking a new name. Our newest employee shared her insight that it would be clear to all of us when we found the right name. After we identified one of our greatest contributions to international development was in forging connections and partnerships, our Operations Manager found the word "Connexus" in a Latin dictionary. It means "a connecting structure," and the word immediately resonated with all of us.
>
> Not only did the course help us identify the new name of our business, the entire process brought us closer together as a team. A few weeks after

the training, an employee was about to leave on a business trip when he learned of an unexpected death in the family. The entire team rallied to support him, using our newfound ability to give empathy and paving the way for him to spend time with his family. Afterwards, he expressed appreciation multiple times for this support. He came back to work fully engaged and even more committed to making a difference in the world.

The big lesson for me is that for a business to be strong, all parts must be operating at full capacity. In most businesses, the employees are the most important part of the equation. The Connection Practice allowed us to see each other as the complex individuals that we are, so that we can function optimally as a cohesive team.

> The Connection Practice allowed us to see each other as the complex individuals we are, so that we can function optimally as a cohesive team.

Self-Empowerment and Coaching for Leaders

When business leaders go a step further and personally adopt the Connection Process as a way to meet their daily challenges, they reap even more benefits. Anita explains:

The Connection Process has helped me in my personal and professional life. I use the process with my seven-year-old son, who has been diagnosed with ADHD. I help him name his feelings so we can work together to address his needs in a constructive way.

I'm also using the Connection Process as a way to
sort out my perceptions when there are problems
on the job. Recently, the staff and I had a misunderstanding regarding our travel per diem policy. The
staff felt upset because they wanted a level of travel
compensation they thought would be fair. At the
same time, I felt resentful and wanted some understanding and appreciation because I had just given
the largest bonuses in company history. I used the
Connection Process to reflect on the situation, and
I saw the issue wasn't really about money; it was
about the need for clear and consistent policies.

I wrote a letter to the staff, acknowledging the break-
down in communication and explaining we would
formalize our policies to prevent further confusion.
I expressed my appreciation for how hard everyone had been working and proposed we go out for
lunch to discuss any other underlying concerns. As a
result, the team agreed to communicate more openly
to avoid misunderstandings in the future.

Staff of AZMJ, now known as Connexus

As the CEO of Rasur Foundation International, I find using the Connection Process helps me manage change, one of the greatest challenges in business. One day I was preparing to meet with a business associate who was working with me on a major change in the relationship between our organizations. John tended to be uncooperative and then would move into blame and try to belittle me. I decided to use the full power of the Connection Process before meeting with him this time. I perused the feelings and needs lists in my workbook and then wrote them down:

My feelings: pessimistic, resentful, suspicious and nervous.

My needs: respect, emotional safety, trust, hope and progress.

Then I wrote down what John's feelings and needs might be: worried and stressed because he needs ease, security, understanding and to matter.

I moved into coherence and the answer came in a flash: *Less is more.* I was surprised at this insight, but as I looked at my notes, I realized I'd planned on covering lots of ground. So I carefully considered how to minimize my words and simplify my request.

In the meeting, I listened respectfully and subtly guessed John's feelings and his needs each time he shared something that distressed him. He responded affirmatively many times during the conversation, saying "Yes, that's right" or "Exactly" or with a nod of his head. The empathy was landing.

When I finally stated my request, this time he didn't try to discredit me. Instead, he said, "Oh sure, we can do that and we can also help you out another way." I felt an authentic, warm connection between us as we said goodbye. Because John had been heard at a deep level, he'd opened up and we moved forward.

Leaders especially benefit from the Connection Process when they are partnered with a coach. I had the opportunity to witness that phenomenon when I was recruiting board members for the Rasur Foundation, our nonprofit organization in Costa Rica. I called up my acquaintance, Carlos Francisco Echeverría, former Minister of Culture and now chief consultant to the national bank. "I'm too busy to get involved right now," he said apologetically, but he wanted to learn more about our program and agreed to meet with me.

When he arrived, I quickly educated him about empathy, coherence and insights; then I asked if he had an issue he'd like to work on. Carlos had just come from a stressful meeting of the board members of the new national stadium. There had been some problems at the stadium, and one journalist in particular had been publically critical about its management.

Carlos peered at the feelings and needs cards on the table and started picking up the feelings that resonated: annoyed, exasperated, resentful and suspicious. I guessed that his needs were to have his intentions understood, to contribute to society, fairness and direct communication. Then I asked him to guess the feelings and needs of the journalist. He imagined that this man felt upset and indignant and needed to have his intentions understood, to contribute to society and to matter. Now Carlos seemed more at ease.

I led Carlos into coherence and asked him to listen for an insight. When he opened his eyes, I asked what had come up. He said, "I didn't have a revelation, but the charge is gone and I know I'll be able to handle it now." Coaching Carlos had taken very little time, but the process had efficiently redirected his emotions. After that experience, Carlos agreed to serve as Vice-President of our board.

Organizational Integration

When organizations invest the time and money to make the Connection Practice a part of their culture, the rewards will multiply. While it provides conflict prevention and resolution, it can also be used for making important financial decisions and strategic planning. Jeff, a management consultant, put it this way:

> It's a different way to get at strategy and problem solving. What I'm used to in my working world is that the problem is presented, and we come to it with different ideas. Sometimes it's hard to come to solutions. The Connection Practice allows me to get clear about the needs I have and consider the needs of the group. With that kind of attention brought to the situation, the practice has shown itself to be a much easier way to come to a solution or strategy that can work.

> The practice has shown itself to be a much easier way to come to a solution or strategy that can work.

Leaders will find that employees embrace this new way of functioning. Kim, a business development specialist, commented, "I enjoyed using coherence and accessing insights during our strategy development exercise."

One of the most difficult situations in business is firing or laying off employees. I remember one instance when I was surprised by a new employee's lack of cooperation. Diane and I had been great friends before she came to work for me at the Rasur Foundation. Now Diane was arguing about each task and seemed to be full of resentment. I needed to let her go, but didn't want to lose her friendship. Using the

Connection Practice, I first worked on myself, identifying my emotions and my need for progress, and guessing at Diane's feelings and needs.

Then I met with Diane and offered her empathy. She opened up, "My father was very strict and authoritarian, so I have issues with authority figures. It's been hard for me to get along with bosses." Her need for autonomy was as deep as my need for progress.

Our next step was to use the Connection Practice to access an insight for moving forward. It came to Diane that she could maintain a perspective of pure choice if she volunteered instead of being an employee. Consequently, she found another way to make a living and has volunteered huge amounts of time to the Rasur Foundation as our Director of Curriculum Development for over 10 years. Her autonomy is intact and we make progress together while enjoying a close friendship.

My success in handling this situation was followed by one where I didn't fare as well. We lost our funding in Costa Rica in 2009 and I needed to lay off almost all our employees, which resulted in hurt feelings and anger. I wasn't masterful enough to prevent this emotional upheaval at the time.

When funds ran out again in 2013, I had learned my lesson and aimed to do it differently. I had to lay off Andrés Jiménez, a young man who had been an incredible asset as our Training Coordinator. As we faced this discouraging situation together, we were able to give each other empathy and honesty, and stay connected. We continue to stay in touch. The Connection Practice gives me the best possibility of sustaining mutual positive regard in these difficult situations.

As a business leader, I need to possess people skills and to access visionary thinking. The practice helps me integrate these two aspects so I can empathize with my colleagues and discern a way forward. This approach improves situations in a surprisingly efficient, and deeply satisfying, way. While we often have to slow down in order to achieve connection, we save time because of the clarity and the cooperation that emerges from the practice. The more we practice it, the better our odds of success become.

Hire the Employee Who Connects

Those who are seeking employment also gain from learning the Connection Practice. George Anders, a contributing editor at *Forbes Magazine* and author of four business books, wrote an article, "The Number One Job Skill in 2020," in which he predicted that empathy would be that skill. The fast-growing occupations that are expected to employ 20% more people in the U.S. include fitness trainers, massage therapists, registered nurses, physical therapists, school psychologists, music tutors, preschool teachers and speech-language pathologists. Anders points out that the common thread among these professions is empathy.[48]

Still there are few educational programs offering empathy training. Ellen, a Rasur, decided to approach the Potomac Massage Training Institute, a prestigious nonprofit organization in Washington, D.C., with the idea of offering the Connection Practice to its students. Ellen and I met with their CEO, Tam Gelman, and their Education Director, Tim Fisher, to explain the practice and explore the possibility of massage therapists obtaining continuing education credits for our courses.

A few weeks later, Tim communicated their plan to make connection a top priority going forward. He said, "We place significant importance on teaching excellent communication skills to our students, especially in light of the somewhat negative impact technology has had on interpersonal connection. The Connection Practice embodies many of the values that are important to our training program. We want to support the practice and make it available at our Institute as well as to the community at large." Now that plan has been put into action.

Since Daniel Goleman made emotional intelligence an everyday term, the concept has infiltrated the business world and is motivating employees to build their social-emotional skills. Goleman advises them, "If your emotional abilities aren't in hand, if you don't have self-awareness, if you are not able to manage your distressing emotions, if you can't have empathy and have effective relationships, then no matter how smart you are, you are not going to get very far."[49]

The Harvard Business Review hailed emotional intelligence as "a ground-breaking, paradigm-shattering idea," one of the most influential business ideas of the decade.[50] Drake Baer, in "Emotional Intelligence Predicts Job Success: Do You Have It?" shares why it matters in the workplace:

> Consider cosmetics giant L'Oréal, which has started to factor emotional intelligence in their hiring process for salespeople. Those who were recruited for their high EQ (emotional intelligence) outsold their peers by over $90,000. On top of that, the high-EQ employees had 63% less turnover than the typically selected sales folk. As this and other studies show, emotional intelligence predicts success for people and the companies they work for.[51]

Now the Connection Practice has given businesses an efficient, powerful way to build social-emotional intelligence in their employees, which ultimately impacts the bottom line.

Connection in Government

Like business, government is faced with the cost of conflict. One way to reduce that cost is through highly effective mediation. Henry Guillén, a lawyer who is an assistant
to the Mayor of Santa Ana in Costa Rica, is a Connection
Practice facilitator and has proposed the integration of the
practice into the *Casa de Justicia* (House of Justice), one
of seventeen mediation centers in the country. He and the
Director, Jeffrey García, plan to teach the Connection Practice to the 15 staff members who serve as community mediators. They will also offer the practice in their community
outreach program. Once this proves successful, the model
will be introduced to the national system of mediation.

Employees in government settings sometimes tell me
they don't feel appreciated as individuals and that the level
of conflict at work is often unbearable. Carolyn, a county
official in Costa Rica, shares how these issues shifted for her
after the Connection Practice was offered at her work site:

> Thanks to my ease in getting along with others, I've
> had the good fortune to meet countless people of all
> social classes, occupations and academic levels.
>
> Finally I did meet a person that I couldn't get
> along with, which was aggravated by the fact that
> this person was my immediate supervisor. At first,
> I assumed it was a matter of rivalry because my
> years in the job were twice hers, but then other
> situations made me doubt that conclusion.
>
> Eventually, I felt very disheartened about my pro-
> fessional position, as my proposals and efforts to
> achieve goals were not valued. My first reaction was
> to run away, but I wasn't sure I could find the same

level of job security, which was important in light of my family responsibilities. I leaned on others and sought their advice, but the discomfort remained.

Several months later, I realized that my gloom was obvious in my treatment of others at work and at home. I had discouragement for breakfast, frustration for lunch, and fatigue for dinner.

One morning at work, I was invited to a Connection Practice course, where I learned to identify my feelings in words and listen inside. The instructor helped me understand that what happens to me does impact me, but I get to decide what that impact will be. This new awareness allowed me to describe this malaise, meet it, confront it and take charge of it.

Since I couldn't leave my job or change the leadership of my department, I decided to apply the Connection Practice. I stopped judging and talking about how much I disliked my supervisor. Instead, I struggled to understand the anguish of my aggressor and to realize her reactions were not about me; they were in reaction to her environment. I listened more, talked less and lowered my expectations of attention and appreciation. Instead, I focused on getting positive outcomes in my work.

From this experience, I came to see that my previous ability to get along with others was not enough. I needed to learn empathy in order to have peace.

Did anything change? Yes. My job is the same and my boss is the same, but my new skill decreased the conflict, especially my internal conflict. Now I'm happier.

Fully implementing the Connection Practice in bureaucratic settings will provide a common framework so employees have a better chance of feeling heard and valued. When employees feel like they belong, employee retention and productivity increase while conflict decreases.

Higher Education

In my Connection Practice Foundations Courses at the University for Peace, I have taught graduate students from around the world. The evaluations I receive fill me with hope. To share just a few:

- Mayn from India: *This course has saved me years of therapy; it has empowered me.*
- Maham from Pakistan: *This practice can be applied in every country in the world.*
- Sunny from the United States: *This practice, and the importance of social-emotional intelligence, would undoubtedly be advantageous for the United States and the many issues it faces.*
- Laticia from Brazil: *I went home with the sensation of a clean soul, something I haven't experienced in a while.*
- Marion from Australia: *This practice can be very important in the field of gender studies, especially regarding gender-based violence.*
- Amit from Nepal: *This practice has exceptionally changed my way of thinking.*
- Destiny from the United States: *To be able to feel the contents of one's own aching heart and questioning mind within a classroom is healing. To be able to connect with one's own emotions, and the emotions of another, is an honor.*

The Connection Practice Foundations Course was the first course in the certificate program of the National Peace Academy, which offers courses throughout the United

States. As interest in the course grew, I introduced it to higher education in other locations like the University of Vermont, the M.K. Gandhi Institute for Nonviolence at the University of Rochester, and a conference for rectors from Latin American universities at the INCAE Business School.

If the Connection Practice was integrated into the academic programs of more universities, the graduates would have a far greater chance of success in their fields. Higher education needs to educate the whole person so we have healthy leaders in every arena of life.

> Higher education needs to educate the whole person so that we have healthy leaders in every arena of life.

Whether a leader works in business, nonprofits, government or higher education, he or she must be an effective change agent, who knows how to connect inside and out. As Robert Kriegel, author of *Sacred Cows Make the Best Burgers*, wrote, "Individuals and organizations that are good react quickly to change. Individuals and organizations that are great create change."[52] Imagine how businesses, nonprofits, governments and higher education institutions will create change when the Connection Practice becomes a part of their culture.

Chapter Summary

1. Most difficulties in organizations stem from strained relationships between employees.
2. Leaders in businesses, nonprofits, government and higher education need people skills and need to access visionary thinking, both of which are sharpened by the Connection Practice.

3. The Connection Practice can be used for conflict prevention and resolution, financial decisions, strategic planning and employee layoffs.

4. When employees are empathic and insightful, they perform their jobs better and stay on the job.

8.

The BePeace® Practice

The Profound Made Practical

Ana signed up at her church to take a BePeace Foundations Course, which is the version of the Connection Practice that is offered to faith-based communities. On the last day of the course, I needed to demonstrate how to use BePeace on an internal conflict, and Ana's hand shot up to volunteer. She took a seat beside me in front of the room, and I asked her to tell us a bit about her inner conflict. She explained:

> In August 1984, my husband and I boarded a plane in San Francisco during my eighth month of pregnancy, bound for the Union of Soviet Social-ist Republics (U.S.S.R.). Jerry's vision was to give birth to our baby in the Soviet Union as a gesture of peace and goodwill between the United States and the U.S.S.R., which were deeply engaged in the Cold War.
>
> Alexander was born in Leningrad on September 6, 1984. When a Soviet newspaper published an article about our journey, the news spread like

wildfire, and the media named Alex the "Peace Baby." After we returned home, however, Jerry lost his job, descended into a deep depression and soon after, the relationship became very painful. We separated a year later and divorced, but remained in conflict for 16 years over custody of Alex.

In 2008, I began writing a book about this life-transforming event. As someone committed to integrity and transparency, I feel torn. It would be disingenuous to share how an idea like a "Peace Baby" can open people's hearts and contribute to world peace without telling the rest of it—the very human story of how unconscious, reactive communication can escalate from conflict into violence.

So my inner conflict is about how much truth to tell and what consequences I might suffer if I tell all. I want to respond to the call of Spirit, but I'm torn up inside about it.

I could see that Ana was distraught and said, "It seems you're feeling torn and worried and scared because you want to be authentic and true to your beliefs, but you need emotional safety, too. Is that right?

"Yes," Ana said, with tears streaming down her face, "and I don't know if people will understand why I'm sharing all this."

"So, are you feeling vulnerable and lonely and needing some reassurance that your intentions will be understood?"

Ana couldn't reply because she was sobbing, and she cried until all the emotion was released. Empathy had opened the wound, it had all gushed out and now she was in a very tender state.

I gently guided Ana into coherence; she listened inside and then opened her eyes. "It seems like Spirit is whispering to me, saying: *There is nothing you can do about something that hasn't happened yet. Write the book, whatever feels authentic and true, and let go of everything else.* I could see the relief in Ana's eyes as she took a big breath and let it out. Her fear had dissolved, and she was comfortable in her own skin once again.

Later, I returned to Ana's church to offer an Advanced BePeace Course, and she signed up as a participant. In this course, the participants put parts of self that are in conflict with one another on the BePeace Path, with the aim of experiencing greater wholeness. I joined Ana's small group to help coach the participants as they walked the path. When it was Ana's turn, she shared her issue:

> I'm fully committed to finishing my book, but as I transcribe my journals from 1984 when I was pregnant, I'm feeling ashamed about some of the things I did back then and worried about how I'll be perceived by readers. I can just imagine criticism like: "*Wow—did you read what she did? What kind of future mother behaves in this way?*" On the other hand, I'm also worried about how much to reveal about my spiritual practices as I imagine that could draw criticism as well. My 60-year-old and 30-year-old selves are in turmoil, so I'm stuck and not getting the book done. I know Spirit is guiding me to write my story, but I just haven't been able to get past this.

As Ana walked the path, she gave self-empathy to her 60-year-old self and then guessed the feelings and needs of her 30-year-old self. This time when she asked for an insight, it came to her that the U.S.S.R. trip wouldn't have happened if that young woman hadn't had a profound faith in the Creator. By accepting her younger self, warts and all, and by giving her "wise woman" the go-ahead to tell the spiritual story, they will birth this book together. A few months later, Ana let me know that she had resigned from her job to work full time on the book and on sharing BePeace.

When people of faith, like Ana, are able to process their inner lives with the help of the BePeace Practice, they can accelerate their spiritual growth and make a greater contribution to humanity.

> With the help of the BePeace Practice, people can accelerate their spiritual growth and make a greater contribution to humanity.

Connection for the Secular and the Sacred

The Connection Practice is not affiliated with any religion, political party or group of any kind. It's neutral and can be learned by any person capable of empathy and insight. Its scientific basis, evidence-based results, and universality have opened the doors to both public and private institutions.

When I first started teaching it, I called it BePeace, as becoming more peaceful is one of the outcomes of this methodology. Many people have found that building their social and emotional intelligence in this way stimulated their spiritual growth. After being exposed to the practice for a week, a University for Peace student from China wrote:

> This method doesn't say anything about religious beliefs. Personally, I found the process of coherence and receiving an insight similar to my

experience of prayer. I wouldn't want this practice to be associated with religion, but it seems like it could strengthen a person's faith. This is another incentive for using it in our lives.

BePeace was a neutral, universal method, but the name was sometimes perceived as "spiritual." As a result, we developed the Connection Practice for our secular courses and kept the BePeace Practice for courses held in faith-based communities. This creates a clear boundary so that everyone feels safe and supported in getting their needs met in our courses. It also gives spiritually oriented individuals the freedom to express themselves in language that is meaningful to them.

Since we were working in Costa Rican public schools that are Catholic by law, I wanted to get a priest's perspective on coherence. I heard about Father Claudio Solano, known for his work in social justice, and I made an appointment with him. That day I spoke the best Spanish I've ever spoken; I demonstrated the emWave and talked about the insights that flow from our hearts. He called other staff members over to try out the software and then walked away to his computer. I thought he'd lost interest. Five minutes later he returned to say, "Here are all the Bible references for 'heart.' This is exactly what we should be teaching in our schools."

Some of the school teachers in Costa Rica have reported that the practice helped them with their prayer life. One little boy in the States said that listening for an insight was like having Jesus in his heart. Shelly, our administrator, calls herself "a good ol' Southern Baptist girl." When I asked her about our methods in relation to her faith, she said, "You teach how to have peace in your life, which has never interfered with my religious beliefs."

When we offer the BePeace Practice to spiritual communities, the participants feel free to interpret their insights from their own frameworks. One graduate, Doreen, explained her insight:

> When I asked what I needed to know about being stuck in unemployment, I saw what I took to be God expressing great appreciation for my gifts. I could feel a warm, welcoming, nurturing presence moving through me. This helped dissolve feelings of tension and the self-judgment that I'm inconsequential.

Sometimes BePeace participants like to use the word "wisdom" rather than "insight" and the word "compassion" rather than "empathy." They see BePeace as a way to access their wisdom and compassion through the heart. The practice is the same, but having the freedom to use the words that work for them is empowering.

I've taught BePeace in churches throughout the United States—Lutheran, Catholic, Congregational, Methodist, Unitarian, Unity, Centers for Spiritual Living and to individuals from almost every religion at the United Nations-mandated University for Peace. When participants realize their belief system is not at risk, and they have the freedom to interpret their insights from their own points of view, they feel right at home.

A Rasur, Denese, shares her experience with a Buddhist who attended her BePeace course:

> In a partner exercise, James shared that, as a practicing Buddhist, he was required to meditate every day for extended periods of time in the morning and evening. He wasn't meditating that often and felt remorseful and guilty about this. His partner

guessed that James might be feeling torn, and James replied, "Not really."

I was coaching these two through the exercise and I wondered if we could find another way to get at the feeling of "torn." So I interrupted and asked James, "Do you think there may be two aspects of yourself fighting to get their needs met—the part that yearns to follow your teachings to further your spiritual growth and the part that might want more freedom and choices?"

"Yes," he said, "now that you say it that way, that's exactly what I'm going through. I guess I am feeling torn between those two parts." His partner helped him explore all his feelings and needs around those two aspects of self.

Then his partner led him into coherence so he could find an insight. Afterwards, James shared his insight: *Giving myself one day per week to not meditate would give me choice and freedom, which would bring more joy and balance into my life.* Releasing the guilt had resulted in a deeper connection with himself. Now he had genuine compassion for the part of him that wanted more freedom. Since compassion is an important part of his Buddhist tradition, he was very excited to have made this discovery.

I've also taught BePeace to people who attend 12-Step groups, which are considered faith-based since they refer to a "higher power." Howard, who has been in a 12-Step program for over 20 years, became a Rasur and introduces the practice to people who are struggling with addictions. He said, "This practice takes what we do in 12 Steps to the next level." Sandy, another 12 Stepper who took a BePeace course, shared, "I got the skill set that transformed me from codependent behavior to unconditional love and acceptance."

Another way I've introduced BePeace is by teaching it to the Peace Ambassadors, a teleseminar class facilitated by James O'Dea and Phillip Hellmich on the Shift Network. This organization reaches faith-based people around the world who want to accelerate positive change. Now I'm offering other BePeace courses with Shift, using the full benefits of their modern-day technology with interactive video and online breakout groups. As we join people throughout the world in this way, the SEL skills that are needed for real change can be developed more efficiently.

Spiritual Benefits of the BePeace Practice

Most religions put an emphasis on forgiveness, and some people have asked me about putting that word on our list of needs. We haven't done that because we know forgiveness is a strategy for peace and connection; it happens naturally when people get reconnected.

In one of my BePeace courses, an elderly gentleman arrived at the church the first day with his son, who was in his fifties. As they walked in, the air fairly crackled with the tension between them, and the son made such a derogatory remark to his father, I cringed. As we gathered in a circle at the conclusion of the course, each participant had a chance to share

> After all these years, I've finally been able to forgive my father and he has forgiven me.

the highlight of their learning. The son said, "After all these years, I've finally been able to forgive my father and he has forgiven me. Now I'm going to get the rest of my family involved in this."

Many people use affirmations for spiritual growth. Insights can easily be transformed into affirmations. Here's one based on the insight I had about my birth experience and my perception of a core unmet need of efficiency that was formed at that time.

Insight: *Show yourself that you're free to be.*
Affirmation: I'm worthy of the time I need and am free to choose how to spend it.

Affirmations simply reinforce the new awareness that you've gained so that it becomes even more transformative.

Music is another spiritual tool that can be used to reinforce insights. After I received the insight *To love everyone, you must love every one,* I found that my mind would still wander back to times I was hurt by my ex-husband. When that happens with him or with anyone that I struggle to hold in positive regard, I turn that insight into a Sunday school song from my childhood:

> I've got the love of (name) down in my heart,
> down in my heart, down in my heart. I've got the
> love of (name) down in my heart, down in my
> heart to stay.

Simple songs like this move me spiritually and help me attain coherence, which anchors the insight soundly in my memory bank.

BePeace Benefits for Faith-Based Communities

Faith-based communities, and their schools, can benefit from the BePeace Practice, just as secular organizations benefit from the Connection Practice. Dr. Laurin Porter, a

retired University of Texas professor, approached the Director of St. Rita's School, Kathleen Krick, about integrating
BePeace into their Catholic school. After hearing about the
social and emotional skills to be had, Kathleen said, "This is
what I've been praying for."

I presented the in-service training to all their teachers,
and they began implementing the BePeace Practice Curriculum in their classrooms. At the end of the year, Dr. Porter
interviewed Kathleen and the teachers. In her report, she
concluded:

> BePeace methodology was an effective tool for
> counseling students, creating a harmonious class-
> room atmosphere, helping students feel calm and
> focused before tests, and giving the students tools
> to understand and take charge of their emotions.

Our next step was to adapt the curriculum to a summer
camp format. Dee Mayes, who serves as our Dallas/Fort
Worth Coordinator and is a retired art teacher, added a
creative arts activity to go with each lesson. The first camp
was held at Unity of Dallas with 24 students, ages 6 to 15,
guided by 11 trained facilitators and directed by a Rasur
Foundation International board member, Lynne Dowler.

The students were a diverse group—culturally, racially and economically. At the end of the camp, the students were invited to write about their experiences. One of the older girls, Mikiyah, wrote, "I've learned how to control my anger. Now I can breathe out my stress and pain so I won't hurt anyone. I've matured over the week."

> Now I can breathe out my stress and pain so I won't hurt anyone.

A younger one made up her own word for expressing it, "Thank you for getting my heart *founded* and peaceful with life." I was delighted to read what Jade, a ninth grader, said; "It was fun and is something that I wish to share later in my life." This is where generational peace begins.

The next BePeace version of summer learning was an interfaith family camp, held at a mosque in Sacramento, California. The 36 participants ranged in ages from 7 to over 70. Denese, the Rasur who led the camp, shared:

> A Muslim mother, whose special-needs teen had presented challenges for other kids, did the BePeace process on stage with me. She shared how vulnerable she felt outside her familiar spiritual community and what a struggle it is to have a safe environment and acceptance for her son. She was so courageous, and with her new awareness from exposure to BePeace, she uncovered her needs to be heard, to be understood and to belong. It was a transformative moment for many of us. After that live demonstration, she and her son were more

tenderly embraced by others; they saw a real person who had universal needs just like theirs.

Jaelan, a teenage boy who attended the camp, shared the value he found in it, "I learned how to take a step back, realize what my feelings are on a deeper level and guess what the other party feels as well." Because of the total immersion in the practice, camps are especially effective in giving children and youth this skill for life.

Spiritual leaders benefit from immersion too. Rev. Elleesabeth Hager took a BePeace Course and afterwards wrote:

> I wanted to thank you for the BePeace process in my life. I've found it immeasurably beautiful in constructing a new life as a chaplain:
>
> I am ordained. I did an internship at a hospital. I have a new website. I'm now a bereavement chaplain and use it with people who are troubled and overwhelmed.
>
> I am finishing my book soon.
>
> Through it all, I've used the process and those lovely worksheets, to realign . . . and to get guidance from Source. It is so simple and so powerful.

Ministers can bring their groups to take the Part 1 Foundations Course at the University for Peace and then tour Costa Rica. Our Director of Curriculum Development, Diane, or I travel with them, providing individual and group coaching, so they can practice what they've just learned. Michelle Deese was delighted with her experience:

> My BePeace tour to Costa Rica and the University for Peace was a dream come true. We learned new methods of connection that led to such a sense of

oneness within our group. Rita Marie and the small-group facilitators taught us how to tap into that space of understanding, compassion, and empathy. We learned how to see situations without judgment, and how to openly express our feelings and needs in a conflict or in celebration. Can I apply this experience in my daily life? Yes, and I have!

After my trip to beautiful Costa Rica, my success with this new practice inspired me to continue with additional classes. I've also volunteered to help bring this to the workplace and to our schools because I see the positive impact that the Connection Practice can have on the world. My relationships and my interactions with people have changed into loving, supportive, healthy connections.

The tours are a fun immersion into nature's paradise while serving as a springboard for quickly learning and applying the practice. Those who participate in tours are also helping to fund the expansion of our mission.

The more a faith-based organization follows through with the practice, the greater the rewards. Rev. Beth Head decided to integrate BePeace into Unity of Melbourne and to reach out to her community as well. After hosting a Foundations Course in 2013 and another in April of 2014, she wrote:

> My church has a vision of building high social-emotional and spiritual intelligence through the BePeace Practice and sharing this with the schools in our county. Whenever issues arise, this unique method efficiently unites our empathy and insight to handle them with ease, harmony and creativity. In this way, it accelerates our individual and collective evolution.

At our center, Rita Marie Johnson has taught two BePeace Foundations Courses and a course to certify our own teachers to offer it. Board members, staff, congregants and community educators have participated, and it has brought us to a more cohesive, confident level.

Our capital campaign for a building at a new location has been less stressful for me because my congregants are more sensitive to my needs. We were also more skilled at giving empathy to members who were resistant to the idea of a move.

Our outreach to the community with the secular version, the Connection Practice, resulted in the Diamond Community School implementing it for all of their students. Members of our congregation are volunteering at the school so that the students have maximum support in learning the practice.

Spiritual communities often need support with their internal conflicts. Rev. Denese Schellink, who is a Rasur and also serves churches as an interim minister, has repeatedly used BePeace for conflict resolution and for helping congregations move through change. As soon as she is hired, she begins offering BePeace courses. As a result, she has a lasting impact even though her time with each church is limited.

Many people have become hurt and disillusioned over the inability of faith-based groups to walk their talk, so they have left those communities. Often their loss of trust has also impacted their hope for a better world; it's a deep wound. People come to places of faith in order to heal and don't expect to be further wounded.

Larry Crabb wrote in his book *Connecting*:

> We have made a terrible mistake! For most of
> the 20th century, we have wrongly defined *soul
> wounds as psychological disorder* and delegated
> their treatment to trained specialists.
>
> Damaged psyches aren't the problem. The problem
> beneath our struggles is a disconnected soul.
>
> I see a healing community as a group of people
> who place connecting at the exact center of their
> purpose and passion.[53]

Just imagine how all faiths will grow in their ability to
nurture congregants as they learn the BePeace Practice.

Chapter Summary

1. The BePeace Practice supports people of all religions
   to grow and to express their insights from their own
   perspective of life.
2. BePeace camps provide immersion in the practice that
   is transformative for children and youth.
3. Internal conflicts within spiritual communities can be
   resolved through empathy and insight.
4. Empathy and insight can help restore trust when people have been hurt or disillusioned by experiences in
   faith-based groups.

9.

Toward a More Connected World

Educating Toward a Connected World Is Realistic

The vision of Rasur Foundation International is a world where every person practices the art of connection and passes this gift on to the next generation. If you've imagined your life changing by practicing connection—and business, higher education, schools, homes and spiritual communities changing as well—then you may find our vision both inspiring and realistic.

We're breaking new ground. In 1981, David Bohm, a physicist, said:

> We are faced with a breakdown of general social order and human values that threatens stability throughout the world. Existing knowledge cannot meet this challenge. Something much deeper is needed, a completely new approach. I am suggesting that the very means by which we try to solve our problems is the problem. The source of our problems is within the structure of thought itself.

This may seem strange because our culture prides itself on thought being its highest achievement.[54]

With the new understanding we've gained about our inner lives, we can solve global problems by taking them to that deeper place where there is only connection and knowing. Some may say this answer is too simplistic to solve complex international issues, yet it's laser-like in getting to the roots of our ills. As Leonardo da Vinci said, "Simplicity is the ultimate sophistication."

Since each person's actions inevitably impact the rest of us, the positive changes each individual experiences from greater connection ripple out into global progress. This could eventually result in better education and reduction of war, poverty, disease, violence and discrimination.

> Since each person's actions inevitably impact the rest of us, the positive changes each individual experiences from greater connection ripple out into global progress.

Enhanced connection will also result in greater empathy for the earth. A woman who had been regularly practicing empathy found herself in an earthquake. Afterwards, as she processed the experience, she got in touch with her fear and her need for safety but was also able to express empathy to the earth for its need for equilibrium.

In our attempts to protect our environment, it's counterproductive to divide into two camps as if we could possibly be "for" or "against" our mutual home. Putting empathy in the forefront of the dialogue, followed up with integrated honesty (remember, this is honesty that takes both my needs and your needs into consideration), could shift us into a more consensual perspective. Then by seeking insights together, we could find some brilliant solutions to our ecological challenges.

Technology is another global arena where we could use the help of the Connection Practice. No doubt technology has made our lives better, but without the wisdom to use it for good, it can be used for destruction. Nuclear weapons are an obvious example. The internet is another; the benefits of connection that it brings are huge, but it's also being used for personal attack, pornography, scams and human trafficking. The poem "Rasur" puts it this way: *Before directing the lightning in the sky, we must first harness the storms in our own hearts.*[55] In other words, advances in powerful technology, without first knowing how to manage our negative emotions, put us and future generations at great risk.

As mentioned in the first chapter, the Connection Practice is not a cure-all for our personal or global ills. At the same time, it would be a huge step in the right direction. I can't imagine any human being, regardless of race, religion or culture, who doesn't want a safer, kinder world in which children can grow and flourish. If we all practiced connection, we would act more frequently out of solid self-esteem rather than from our insecurities. We would know how to keep everyone's needs on the table and seek intuitive solutions for getting those needs met. Persevering with this approach would take us beyond the limits of either/or thinking and into the realm of both/and possibilities. Imagine what this type of thinking could do to reverse the polarization of the U.S. Congress so that mutual understanding and creativity could pave the way to progress.

This path is simple but it's not easy. Learning to connect is a lifelong journey and has been the most challenging goal in my life. I still don't consider myself a master at it, but I'm a much improved version of the "me" that existed 10 years ago. My growth is real and my happiness is steady. Because of that, I know every human being has the capacity to change at depth.

I've taught the Connection Practice to six-year-olds and to elders as old as 89. They were all able to get it. Participants in Connection Practice courses that I've taught in countries other than Costa Rica and the United States have all embraced it. Having passed the test of being cross-generational and cross-cultural, all that remains is to deliver it to those who are willing to learn it.

At the same time, I'm not naïve about the challenges of teaching connection throughout the world. There are traditions and beliefs embedded in cultures that create ongoing generational disconnection and suffering. These patterns of thinking won't disappear overnight. Diane went to the Congo to teach the Connection Practice, where she found the concept of submission so entrenched that participants had difficulty grasping the idea of keeping everyone's needs on the table. She tells this story:

> When it was Yvonne's turn to walk the Connection Path, she said her conflict was with her father-in-law. After her husband died, her father-in-law told her she didn't deserve the husband's property. She felt hurt and sad over this as she needed fairness and support.

> When Yvonne came to the step on the path of practicing empathy for her father-in-law, I asked her to identify what her father-in-law saw that made him think she didn't deserve the property. She revealed that after her husband died, she got sick and went back to her family's home. When she returned, her

father-in-law told her she was to marry her husband's brother (a custom common in her culture). When she wouldn't do it, he told her she didn't deserve the property.

When Yvonne came to the last step of the path, her request to her father-in-law was, "I'm willing to offer my obedience. Are you willing to accept it?"

My conclusion is that people keep going back to submission because it's the only paradigm they know. Even though we have a how-to for changing this paradigm, it's going to take huge amounts of training to get it across.

While Diane struggled with the domination-submission dynamic in that culture, she also had some success. One participant shared, "The Connection Practice will allow me to change the energy in me that is 'against' to energy that is 'for' by offering empathy to others. I will no longer lack peace because, from now on, I know we belong to each other."

Another Congolese participant took the course and then attended a Connection Practice group. He explained he'd broken up with his fiancée because she insisted that he go to her church. When he used the language of feelings and needs and concluded with his need to be seen for who he was, she accepted that he didn't need to change his religion. They got back together.

Despite the barriers, change occurs when we fully implement tools that work. If we continue to educate for connection, results have shown that we can realistically expect a change for the better. It will take ongoing commitment to teach this practice throughout the world. However, the practice deserves this commitment because it brings us together, regardless of our perspectives, and imbues life with camaraderie, meaning and exhilarating progress.

> If we continue to educate for connection,
> results have shown that we can realistically
> expect a change for the better.

Social Change and Restorative Justice

When I teach graduate students at the University for Peace, I'm continually inspired by their papers. Many of them want to return to their countries and implement the Connection Practice in their educational and legal systems. Here are some examples of social change they envision with the Connection Practice in their countries:

- Juliet envisions training politicians, teachers and school children, social workers, nonprofit leaders, and grassroots communities in Uganda, which is recovering from war and is seeking peace, justice and reconciliation.
- Bin Li sees the potential for changing China from an obedience-based culture to a culture of empathy.
- Yves from Rwanda believes the practice can make a significant difference in his country as they heal from genocide.
- Ori can imagine her country, Israel, moving from a militaristic state to one that brings peace to the world.
- Kashia sees the practice as essential in natural disaster relief efforts in the United States.
- Jun wants to see the practice begin at the grassroots level in an effort to change the educational system and reduce suicides in Japan.

University for Peace graduate students and Rasurs

Lindsey, a University for Peace student from Canada, wrote a paper on Communication for Development that revealed a new arena where the Connection Practice can fit. The United Nations Children's Fund (UNICEF) defines communication for development as "a systematic, planned and evidence-based strategic process to promote positive and measurable individual behavior and social change that is an integral part of development programs, policy advocacy and humanitarian work."[56] What might happen, Lindsey proposed, if the Connection Practice was a part of that strategic process?

United Nations Resolution A/RES/52/13 states that the UN is seeking a set of values, attitudes, modes of behavior and ways of life that reject violence and prevent conflicts by tackling their root causes to solve problems through dialogue and negotiation among individuals, groups and nations.[57] It appears that Rasur Foundation International and the United Nations are in sync; we have similar goals, and the Connection Practice efficiently gets to the root causes they want to address. The practice is an engine for positive social change, yet we know that connection is not the end-all in a conflict; right action must follow.

Restorative justice is an approach to right action that is in alignment with connection, as it focuses on the needs of the

victims and the offenders. Through dialogue among these
parties, offenders are encouraged to take responsibility for
their actions and make amends. Restorative justice also provides appropriate help for the offender in an effort to avoid
future offenses. According to the Smith Institute's report
"Restorative Justice: The Evidence," this type of conflict
resolution shows the highest rate of victim satisfaction and
offender accountability.[58]

Restorative justice flows from a natural impulse to be
connected. Its strength is that the structure engenders a balance of empathy and honesty, forgiveness and accountability. The outcome is healing and learning rather than revenge
and punishment. Coupling the Connection Practice with
restorative justice will take social change to a new level and
will help accomplish the global progress we are pursuing.

Inside Out, Bottom Up, Top Down and All Around

We offer the Connection Practice to all levels of society so
it can spread in all directions: This is accomplished through
Rasurs who have completed a training track and been certified by Rasur Foundation International.[k]

> We offer the Connection Practice
> to all levels of society so it can
> spread in all directions.

Inside Out—We begin by uniting the empathy and insight
within ourselves, as all true change starts inside each of us.

Bottom Up—We offer the practice at the grassroots level

---

k. To learn more, go to rasurinternational.org/training-track to students, teachers and parents in the schools and to the general public through teleseminars, courses, retreats, tours, and coaching.

On our website, we also offer the Connection Experience, an online course that also includes sessions with a certified coach. Anyone going through a difficult situation should give it a try.

Our planet is crisscrossed by millions of lines of communication that can be used for heart-to-heart connection. Imagine those lines being used by people all over the world who are hurting and who are being guided by a coach to discover their own empathy and insight. In this way, our fragmented world can be re-connected, one heart at a time.

Top Down—For social-emotional learning to have maximum impact on society, it must be supported by national leaders. We did our best to make that happen in Costa Rica. I share that story here with the hope that it will inspire other countries to follow suit.

In 2007, I partnered with Alexandra Kissling, Vice President of the Rasur Foundation of Costa Rica and Vice President of the Association of Businesses for Development, to get support at the highest level for institutional integration of the Connection Practice. We began with a presentation to Vice-Minister of Education Alejandrina Mata. She was surprised by the science and power of the method and, afterwards, gave the green light to the leaders in the ministry to move ahead with us. Consequently, teachers came to our 40-hour course on paid time, which counted toward their continuing education requirement necessary for receiving a salary increase.

This was a good start, but we knew social-emotional learning needed to be entrenched in the government so it would survive changes of leadership. Alexandra and I met with President Oscar Arias, Nobel Peace Prize laureate, to explain our methodology and explore ideas. He was open to our innovative approach to peace through SEL programs.

After this meeting, I thought further about how to establish infrastructure that supports social-emotional learning. I'd heard about the Global Alliance for Ministries and Departments for Peace, whose aim was to establish such ministries and departments in every country. Costa Ricans identify with peace because they abolished their army in 1948. I wondered if a Ministry for Peace in Costa Rica could be a vehicle for promoting SEL programs.

After researching this possibility, Alexandra and I wrote a proposal for a Ministry for Peace and, in 2006, had a meeting with the Minister of the Presidency, Rodrigo Arias; the Minister of Justice, Laura Chinchilla; and the Minister of Education, Leonardo Garnier. They agreed with our idea to integrate a Ministry for Peace into the Ministry of Justice, so it would be renamed the "Ministry for Justice and Peace." The purpose of this Ministry for Peace would be the creation of a national system for the promotion of peace and peaceful citizen coexistence. Minister Chinchilla would be in charge of writing the bill, and we would be consulted on it.

After the bill was introduced in the Legislative Assembly, we began to lobby for it and were disappointed when it didn't pass right away. After that, I got involved in the Global Alliance,[1] and Minister Chinchilla appointed me to represent Costa Rica at their summit in Japan in 2007. While at the Global Alliance Summit, I taught a workshop on the Connection Practice and proposed that Costa Rica sponsor the next summit in 2009. The alliance agreed and, when I returned to Costa Rica, Minister Chinchilla

---

1. www.gamip.org

confirmed that the Costa Rican government would host that event and the Rasur Foundation would convene it.

Confident that our bill would pass, Alexandra and I approached the Ministry of Justice with the idea of uniting peace-oriented organizations in Costa Rica. We wanted to prepare them to work hand in hand with the new ministry. Milena Sanabria, Vice-Minister of Justice, agreed to move forward on this initiative. The first meeting of *Red de Paz* (network of peace) was convened by the Vice-Minister and attended by representatives from 58 nonprofit organizations at Rasur Foundation headquarters in June 2009.

Now the Global Alliance Summit was only a month away, and we were hoping that the Ministry for Peace bill would pass before this event began. Alexandra stepped up her lobbying efforts and discovered there was an outspoken congressman who opposed it. Prior to a meeting with him, she and I talked about the importance of giving him empathy and staying coherent as they interacted. Alexandra walked her talk and, during the meeting, the congressman shifted to a "yes" position. On August 19, 2009, the vote was finally taken, and the bill passed without opposition. Costa Rica became the third country in the world[m] to establish this infrastructure.

In September, we offered a Connection Practice course (40 hours) as the pre-summit activity with 38 participants from 10 countries. The course set a harmonious tone for the rest of the summit. The most touching moment was at the opening ceremony at the National Auditorium. One of our Connection Practice students, a first grader named Ashlee Rodriguez, led the 500-strong crowd into coherence. You

---

m. The Solomon Islands has had a Ministry of Reconciliation, Peace and National Unity since 2006. Nepal established a Ministry of Peace and Reconciliation in 2007.

could have heard a pin drop as the audience followed her soft, clear voice into their hearts.

President Oscar Arias gave the opening keynote and emphasized the role of Costa Rica's new ministry: "The task is only just starting; the creation of a Ministry for Peace . . . is not the final achievement, but merely the making of a road to achieve sustainable order that would allow resolution of human conflicts without violence." A framed letter from the Dalai Lama, endorsing the purpose of the summit, was also read to the audience; it is now read at the Global Alliance Summit each year.

Top-down support for social-emotional learning in Costa Rica is making a difference. The Ministry for Justice and Peace has built a Civic Center for Peace. This center includes areas for sport and recreation, a music school, performing arts space, a House of Justice for mediation, a child care center, a library and a community center. The ministry plans to build six more such centers as a strategy to "combat violence and promote social inclusion for our children, adolescents and youth."[59] The Ministry is also supporting the National Alternative Dispute Resolution Office by offering training for the office's mediators. These mediators can help prevent conflicts from going to court.[60]

Establishing a ministry or department of peace is one way to institutionalize social and emotional learning. Other countries may need to find a different strategy. Their first step will be to secure the interest of influential leaders in pursuing this aim. We've found that engaging each leader in a coaching session or course is the most effective way to generate heartfelt commitment to SEL.

In 2007, Minister Chinchilla came to our headquarters to learn about the Connection Practice program in the schools. As she was leaving, she said, "I want to take one of your courses." As it turned out, before we could get her into a course, she declared her candidacy and became the first female president of Costa Rica in May 2010. Now that she's finished her term, we hope she'll have time to take a course. In the meantime, we've trained other leaders in Costa Rica.

Nancy Marín served as Director of our Costa Rica program and now works as Adviser to the Minister of Human Development and Social Inclusion. She has trained close to 1,000 people in the Connection Practice, and she advocates for national implementation of the method in the Costa Rican school system. She says:

> It's easy to teach the Connection Practice to children because they have a natural capacity to connect with their emotions and inner wisdom. As we grow up, we lose that ability, so when we learn to connect, it's like rediscovering something we already knew. This soft skill is essential for our social development and needs to be included in our educational system.

Now our courses for international leaders end with a call to action: find the way to offer Connection Practice training to every willing teacher in your country.

In every country, common knowledge is passed from generation to generation. In Costa Rica, the children all soon learn the rules of soccer. As their leaders integrate the Connection Practice into the schools and into government institutions, the steps of the practice can become common knowledge too. When this takes place in countries all over the world, connection will be the norm rather than the exception.

All Around—Connection applies to every segment of the population, so we refer to all other categories as the "all around." We train business people, staff from nonprofit organizations and members of faith-based communities, all of which are essential in developing a culture of compassion and innovation. One example of our "all around" approach is evolving in Guadalajara, Mexico where an organization, Corente, is integrating the Connection Practice into its social service projects in alliance with leaders from nonprofits, universities, government and business.

The how-to of connection is sure to catch on, yet it could take a long time to seep into the global culture. With the help of the media, it will catch on like wildfire. Most of the media is focused on what's wrong, and what's wrong seems to expand when given attention. The same is true when the media highlights stories where this simple practice has changed the course of lives—positive attention expands our reach. This is one of the steps needed to create a quantum leap in global progress.

The Experience of Connection as Common Ground

As our "inside out, bottom up, top down and all around" model continues to expand, we are creating a world where we can evolve without causing unnecessary pain to each other. Every conscious choice we make to connect with ourselves and others moves us toward self-actualization, while every unconscious choice we make, out of fear, debilitates our hopes and dreams.

The Connection Practice has proven to be a truly universal skill for building social-emotional intelligence, the measure of how you handle yourself and your feelings and how well you interact with others. Without social-emotional skills, establishing peace around the world is an impossible dream. With them, peace becomes an achievable way of life.

Yumi, the Rasur who is spreading the Connection Practice in Japan, puts it this way, "After September 11, 2011, I launched the Global Peace Campaign to find alternative solutions to the war on terror, but I did not know how. Now I realize the Connection Practice is the tool I want to create peace in and around me, and eventually peace on earth when we all possess the skills of a Rasur."

Speaking of peace in this way doesn't mean that people who learn the Connection Practice are against armies. Until human beings learn to connect as a way to get their needs met, there will be times when the protective use of force is necessary. Our participants from the military find value in gaining the skills of empathy and insight. Dottie Henderson, a retired army colonel, said, "If you want peace and harmony within and without, the Connection Practice is for you."

Police can also benefit from learning the practice. News media show us ongoing examples of perpetrators and police officers being killed when other options for conflict resolution might have been used. These incidents stimulate us to look at another possibility for law enforcement—teaching the police how to give empathy first and use force second. Just as with the military, there will be times when the protective use of force is necessary, as we need boundaries that don't allow others to physically hurt people. But it's not hard to imagine reducing the unnecessary use of force if police were well trained in the Connection Practice. On the other hand, whole communities could be trained in the Connection Practice so that police would rarely be put in jeopardy.

No matter your occupation, chances are you could use more peace in your life. In our busy world, many people seem to be running on empty. The Connection Practice is like filling up with peace at the gas tank—a renewable energy that is always available to you. No tool is infallible, as it depends on the consciousness and skill of the person who is using it and the receptivity of others involved. At least now we have a tool that is custom made for integrating our inner strengths while giving us practical answers to living in the world. Simply put, connection makes us feel calm and loved so we can be at our best in creating a world that works for everyone.

The greatest benefit over many years is a deeper trust in the mystery of life and more spontaneous joy in my heart. Now I can see myself as I am and evoke my empathy and insight to empower myself. I see others as they are and can help them tap into their empathy and insight. I see life as it is, delighting in the evolution that flows from our collective empathy and insight, and experiencing growth from the transcendent nature of life itself. Albert Camus said, "In the middle of winter, I at last discovered that there was in me an invincible summer."[61] The Connection Practice led me to that lasting summer.

As more of us improve in our ability to connect at this level, hope is flourishing, a hope not founded upon intellectual inquiry or childish fantasy, but on a solid, grounded expectation that life can get better. This is the nitty-gritty stuff that makes violence preventable and glorious visions attainable.

> This is the nitty-gritty stuff that makes violence preventable and glorious visions attainable.

One of our Connection Practice graduates told me that the course had changed his perception of reality. Buckminster Fuller, the scientist and visionary, said, "In order to change an existing paradigm, you don't struggle and try to change the problematic model. You create a new model and make the old one obsolete." Can you imagine people at all levels of society recognizing the *experience* of connection—a new model—as their common ground?

Chapter Summary

1. Each individual's progress toward connection ripples out into global progress.
2. Empathy and insight can help resolve global issues, such as use of technology, social change and justice.
3. Empathy and insight must be attained inside out, bottom up, top down and all around for a more connected world.

10.

A New Beginning

Now that we've fully explored the value of connection, I encourage you to start learning this skill and never stop. Over time, you'll find deep contentment in the practice as it will give you comfort in situations that previously felt comfortless.

In my family, what seemed comfortless was the fact that we didn't know how to heal emotional pain. We shoved it under the rug and kept on going. I remember sitting at the kitchen table with my grandmother after my grandfather died. With a tear in her eye, she lamented, "I was cold to your grandfather and I have no idea why." She was mourning her behavior, and I ended up crying with her. Now, I imagine that something painful had happened in her past and her amygdala was impacted by it; she had formed a cold defense without knowing how to warm up her heart again. She'd never found her way out of that prison, and now it was too late to express her love to her husband.

My dad followed a similar path as he handled his shyness by stuffing his feelings. He used to say, "Don't follow your feelings—think." Counter to that expression, he would become depressed at times and sit brooding in a chair in the living room. His feelings were controlling him because he was unable to name them or express them.

What saved Dad was his willingness to keep on learning. When he came to live with me in Costa Rica in his late seventies, he observed our work and came to understand his inner life. He learned to embrace his feelings and needs and found he could achieve heart-brain coherence as a way to function at his very best. We lived together and our relationship deepened through this new way of processing whatever was coming up in life.

Dad became an advocate of the Connection Practice and, in an email to his grandchildren, wrote, "This skill wasn't available when I was your age. It's better than a college education. I have hope that your lives will be successful and happy. This skill can do it for you!" He was intent on breaking a generational pattern in our family that had limited our enjoyment of life.

Dad broke out of his lifelong pattern of shyness and would start conversations about the Connection Practice with strangers, even asking them to support the work. I loved to hear him talk passionately about the vision we now shared of a connected world. The deep acknowledgement and understanding I received in those moments was priceless—it was world-class empathy.

In 2011, Dad attended a conference to launch Connection Practice trainers, and he got to know them better. We ended the event with an appreciation walk; each person took a turn walking down the middle of two lines of trainers, as they whispered words of appreciation in that person's ears. My white-haired, 86-year-old father, Carl Johnson, participated with the rest of us, reaching into each person's heart with his words.

When it was his turn to walk down the line, each trainer spoke softly to him at length, while the others stood by with tears rolling down their cheeks. When they finished, the group gathered into a tight circle, arm in arm, and spontaneously rocked back and forth, deeply connecting with Dad. This was the greatest victory in his life: He had overcome his lack of confidence and was finally at home connecting with others.

May the ability of every human being to get connected free us of needless emotional pain and inspire us to make a new beginning like my father did. With all the good will that's in us, let's create a worldwide culture of connection. We want to be the change we wish to see in the world. Now we know how.

For a New Beginning

In out-of-the-way places of the heart,
Where your thoughts never think to wander,
This beginning has been quietly forming,
Waiting until you were ready to emerge.

For a long time it has watched your desire,
Feeling the emptiness growing inside you,
Noticing how you willed yourself on,
Still unable to leave what you had outgrown.

It watched you play with the seduction of safety
And the gray promises that sameness whispered,
Heard the waves of turmoil rise and relent,
Wondered would you always live like this.

Then the delight, when your courage kindled,
And out you stepped onto new ground,
Your eyes young again with energy and dream,
A path of plenitude opening before you.
Though your destination is not yet clear
You can trust the promise of this opening;
Unfurl yourself into the grace of beginning
That is at one with your life's desire.

Awaken your spirit to adventure;
Hold nothing back, learn to find ease in risk;
Soon you will be home in a new rhythm,
For your soul senses the world that awaits you.

—John O'Donohue

Get Started Connecting Today

We want to make it easy for you to improve your connection skills. You'll find a guide and resources below for that purpose. You can also contact us at:

Rasur Foundation International
e-mail: info@rasurinternational.org
www.rasurinternational.org
Phone: 469-708-7804
Address: PO Box 170055, Irving, Texas 75017

Overcome the Fear of Looking Inside

The first step to getting completely connected is to overcome any resistance you have to regularly looking inside yourself. Knowing what you are looking for—feelings and needs and insights—makes inner work a lot less intimidating. Would you like to try it? Using the feelings and needs lists on pages 48, 49 and 50, fill out the Connection Process worksheet on the next page.

The Connection Process Worksheet

1. My challenge (include judgments and blame if needed) or my celebration:

2. My feelings:

3. My met or unmet needs:

(If no one else is involved, go to step 6.)
4. Other person's/people's feelings:

5. Other person's/people's met or unmet needs:

6. Now I do a Heart-Brain Insight as follows:
   • Quick Coherence (heart focus, heart breathing, heart feeling of appreciation)
   • I ask, "What do I need to know?"
   • My insight:

   • How I will act on my insight:

Get the Habit Going

If you want to develop the daily habit of connection, *The Connection Process Daily Workbook* is the best support in getting that habit rooted in your routine. Even if you don't practice every day, some attention to it is definitely better than none.

You can also order a pack of feelings and needs cards. Instructions come with the cards so you can start using them immediately with friends and family members. You can also order GROK cards for children who can't yet read or those students who struggle with words and relate most easily to pictures.

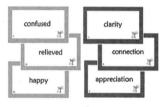

Another way to go about this is to start guessing the feelings and needs of others as you encounter them in your daily life. You'll be amazed at what happens. At the same time, if you're going to try this out on family members, ask if they're willing to help you practice so they don't feel threatened by this new approach.

The quickest, most reliable way to learn coherence is with the emWave Pro or Inner Balance from the Institute of HeartMath. Rasur Foundation International (RFI) is a distributor of HeartMath products so you can order any of their products through us. When you do that, you receive the same price that you would on the HeartMath website,

---

Workbooks, Feelings and Needs Cards, GROK Cards and HeartMath products are available at rasurinternational.org/store.

---

even when they offer special sales. By ordering through RFI, the commission goes to our nonprofit work. Write to info@ rasurinternational.org to order any HeartMath product you can't find in the online shop.

If You Want to Dive into the Experience

If you want to connect with another person to get a taste of the practice, you can have a Connection Experience with a certified coach. You can also contact a Rasur in your area for a coaching session. You'll find a list of Rasurs on the website.

Perhaps you'd like to hear more about the Connection Practice and be able to ask questions. You can do that by signing up for a free teleseminar with me.

To immerse yourself in the practice, it's best to take a course. These courses have been approved for college credit and for continuing education credit for various professions in many states. After you take a course, you'll want to find a partner or practice group and continue honing your skill.

Another way to immerse yourself and learn the practice quickly is to take a tour to Costa Rica. There you'll take a course and then see this beautiful country while practicing your new skill with others in your group.

Find a coach:
rasurinternational.org
/trainers-coaches
Find a teleseminar:
rasurinternational.org
/teleseminars
Find a course:
rasurinternational.org
/find-a-course
Find a tour:
rasurinternational.org
/costa-rican-tours

Passing It Forward

If you want to spread the word about the value of connection, you can:

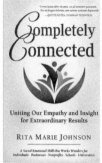

- initiate a book study of *Completely Connected*, using the book study guide in the back of this book
- gift this book to leaders, educators, business people, parents, churches— and any others who you think would benefit from it
- suggest to your school, university, nonprofit organization, business, church or government that they contact us for a course or retreat
- connect us with influential leaders

We want every person who desires to take a course to be able to do so, no matter what their economic level may be. Donations and grants will make it possible to offer scholarships to Connection Practice courses around the world. If you want to help, you can:

- make a donation at rasurinternational.org/donate
- connect us with potential donors by writing info@rasurinternational.org
- assist in grant writing

> We want every person who desires to take a course to be able to do so.

> For more copies of *Completely Connected*, go to rasurinternational.org/store.

Getting Started with the
Connection Practice at School

Are you excited about introducing the Connection Practice at a school? Here's how:

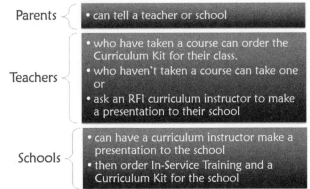

Parents — • can tell a teacher or school

Teachers — • who have taken a course can order the Curriculum Kit for their class.
• who haven't taken a course can take one or
• ask an RFI curriculum instructor to make a presentation to their school

Schools — • can have a curriculum instructor make a presentation to the school
• then order In-Service Training and a Curriculum Kit for the school

There are two options for in-service training at a school:

1. Connection Practice In-Service Training presented by a certified curriculum instructor (six hours). Then the instructor provides support in implementing the curriculum in the classroom.

2. Part 1, Connection Practice Foundations Course (12 hours) presented by a certified curriculum instructor with an additional four hours of curriculum instruction. The teachers will be able to implement the curriculum on their own.

The school can also ask the instructor to provide a course for parents, an after-school program or a summer camp for families.

To find a curriculum instructor, go to
rasurinternational.org/trainers-coaches.

Getting Started on the Professional Track

Don't underestimate the power you have to make a difference after learning the Connection Practice. You can positively impact people every day just by modeling it. Many of those who learn the Connection Practice also want to pass it on to others in a structured way.

> Don't underestimate the power you have to make a difference after learning the Connection Practice.

There are over 100 certified trainers in the Bahamas, Canada, Costa Rica, Japan, New Zealand, Puerto Rico, and the United States at this time. Soon there will be many more as people from Mexico, Colombia and other countries are getting started on the training track. As they master the dance of empathy and insight, they gain an inner authority that makes their courses rich and impactful.

The training track for becoming certified as a trainer or coach is:

1. **Take the Connection Practice Foundations Course** (either the 32-hour course or Parts 1, 2 and 3, of 12 hours each).

2. **Take the Facilitator Course and facilitate a small group within a Foundations Course.** For a 32-hour course, an 8-hour facilitator training is required, and for a Part 1, 2, or 3 course, a 3-hour facilitator training is required.

3. **Take the Rasur Certification Course** (hours based on student's level of mastery).

After becoming a Rasur, if you want to offer in-service training in schools, you can take additional training to become a certified curriculum instructor.

Notes

1. "Quick Coherence Technique." Institute of HeartMath. Accessed January 13, 2015. heartmath.com/quick-coherence -technique.

2. Fein, Robert A., Bryan Vossekuil, William S. Pollack, Randy Borum, William Modzeleski, Marisa Reddy. "Threat Assessment in Schools: A Guide to Managing Threatening Situations and to Creating Safe School Climates." U.S. Department of Education, Office of Elementary and Secondary Education, Safe and Drug-Free Schools Program and U.S. Secret Service, National Threat Assessment Center, 2002:12. Accessed January 13, 2015. www.secretservice .gov/ntac/ssi_guide.pdf.

3. Brown, Brené. *Daring Greatly: How the Courage to Be Vulnerable Transforms the Way We Live, Love, Parent, and Lead.* New York: Penguin Group (USA) Inc., 2012: 145.

4. Brenes Mesén, Roberto. *Rasur o Semana de Esplendor.* Heredia: Trejos Hermano, 1998.

5. Goleman, Daniel. *Emotional Intelligence: 10th Anniversary Edition; Why It Can Matter More Than IQ.* New York: Bantam Dell, 2006.

6. "HeartMath System FAQs." Institute of HeartMath. Accessed January 13, 2015. heartmath.org/index.php?tmpl=component &option=com_content&id=156.

7. Childre, Doc, Howard Martin, and Donna Beech. *The Heart-Math Solution.* New York: Harper Collins, 1999: 37–38.

8. "The Amygdala: Definition, Role & Function." Education Portal. Accessed January 13, 2015. education-portal.com/academy/ lesson/the-amygdala-definition-role-function.html.

9. Institute of HeartMath, *The Resilient Educator Trainer Manual.* Boulder Creek: Institute of HeartMath; 2006:17–18.

10. Rozman, Deborah, Rollin McCraty, and Jeffrey Goelitz. "The Role of the Heart in Learning and Intelligence: A Summary of Research and Applications with Children." Institute of HeartMath, 1998; 6. Accessed January 15, 2015. heartmathbenelux.com/doc/ Role_of_the_Heart%20in %20learning%20and%20intelligence.pdf.

11. McCraty, Rollin, Dana Tomasino, Mike Atkinson, Pam Aasen, and Stephanie J. Thurik. "Improving Test-Taking Skills and Academic Performance in High School Students Using HeartMath Learning

Enhancement Tools." Institute of HeartMath, 2000. Accessed January 15, 2015. heartmathbenelux.com/doc/education %20improving-test-taking.pdf.

12. Bradley, Raymond Trevor, Rollin McCraty, Mike Atkinson, Lourdes Arguelles, Robert A. Rees, and Dana Tomasino. "Reducing Test Anxiety and Improving Test Performance in America's Schools: Summary of Results from the TestEdge National Demonstration Study." Institute of HeartMath, 2007: 4. Accessed January 15, 2015. heartmathbenelux.com/doc/Tends_Summary_Results%202007.pdf.

13. Bradley, Raymond, Mike Atkinson, Robert A. Rees, Dana Tomasino, and Patrick Galvin. "Facilitating Emotional Self-Regulation in Preschool Children: Efficacy of the Early HeartSmarts Program in Promoting Social, Emotional and Cognitive Development." Institute of HeartMath. 2009. Accessed January 15, 2015. heartmath.org/templates/ihm/downloads/pdf/research/publications/facilitating-emotional-self-regulation-in-preschool-children.pdf.

14. Lloyd, Anthony, David Brett, and Keith Wesnes. "Coherence Training In Children with Attention-Deficit Hyperactivity Disorder: Cognitive Functions and Behavioral Changes." *Alternative Therapies*, 16, no.4 (2010): 34–42. Accessed January 15, 2015. newvisionwilderness.com/assets/nvw/userfiles/file/Coherence-Children%20ADHD_Lloyd.pdf.

15. Subramaniam, Karuna, John Kounios, Todd B. Parrish, and Mark Jung-Beeman. "A Brain Mechanism for Facilitation of Insight by Positive Affect." *Journal of Cognitive Neuroscience* 21, no. 3 (March 3, 2009): 415–432. doi:10.1162/jocn.2009.21057.

16. "Physics: Discovery and Intuition." Physics Intuition Applications Corporation. 2003. Accessed January 14, 2015. p-i-a.com/Magazine/Issue19/Physics_19.htm.

17. Samples, Bob. *The Metaphoric Mind: A Celebration of Creative Consciousness*. Boston: Addison Wesley Longman Publishing Company, 1976: 26.

18. "Defining Critical Thinking." Foundation for Critical Thinking. Accessed January 13, 2015. http://www.criticalthinking.org/pages/defining-critical-thinking/410.

19. Frankl, Viktor. *Man's Search for Meaning*. Boston: Beacon Press, 2006.

20. McCraty, Rollin, Bob Barrios-Choplin, Deborah Rozman, Mike Atkinson, and Alan Watkins. "The Impact of a New Emotional Self-Management Program on Stress, Emotions, Heart Rate Variability, DHEA and Cortisol." *Integrative Physiological and*

Behavioral Science 33, no. 2 (April–June 1998): 159–160. Accessed January 14, 2015. heartmathbenelux.com/doc/DHEA_Cortisol _Study.pdf.

21. Wechsler, Amy. *The Mind-Beauty Connection: 9 Days to Less Stress, Gorgeous Skin, and a Whole New You.* New York: Free Press, 2008: 4 and 132.

22. Solon, Olivia. "Compassion over empathy could help prevent emotional burnout." Accessed January 15, 2015. wired.co.uk. July 2012. wired.co.uk/news/archive/2012-07/12 /tania-singer-compassion-burnout.

23. Lieberman, Matthew D., Naomi I. Eisenberger, Molly J. Crockett, Sabrina M. Tom, Jennifer H. Pfeifer, and Baldwin M. Way. "Putting Feelings into Words: Affect Labeling Disrupts Amygdala Activity in Response to Affective Stimuli." *Psychological Science* 18, no. 5 (May 2007): 421–428. doi: 10.1111/j.1467-9280.2007 .01916.x.

24. Lamm, Claus, C. Daniel Batson, and Jean Decety. "The Neural Substrate of Human Empathy: Effects of Perspective-taking and Cognitive Appraisal." *Journal of Cognitive Neuroscience* 19, no. 1 (January 2007): 42–58. doi:10.1162/jocn.2007.19.1.42.

25. Brown, Brené, *The Gifts of Imperfection: Let Go of Who You Think You're Supposed to Be and Embrace Who You Are.* Center City: Hazelden Publishing, 2010: 17.

26. Kennelly, Stacey. "Educating for Empathy." Greater Good Science Center. July 18, 2012. Accessed January 15, 2015. greatergood .berkeley.edu/article/item/educating_for_empathy.

27. Thoreau, Henry David, *Walden.* 1906:11. Accessed January 15, 2015. walden.org/documents/file/Library/Thoreau /writings/Writings1906/02Walden/Walden01Economy.pdf.

28. Pennebaker, James. "Writing to Heal." University of Texas at Austin. March 15, 2005. Accessed January 15, 2015. http://www .utexas.edu/features/2005/writing.

29. "Ask a UT psychologist (emotional well-being)--James Pennebaker." YouTube Video, 3:15. Posted by The University of Texas at Austin, August 1, 2011. Accessed January 16, 2015. http://youtu.be /tsV_oQC7n8k.

30. Lieberman, 2007.

31. Lamm, 2007.

32. Subramaniam. 2009.

33. Chida, Yoichi, Mark Hamer, Jane Wardle, and Andrew Steptoe. "Do Stress-Related Psychosocial Factors Contribute to Cancer

Incidence and Survival?" *Nature Reviews Clinical Oncology* 5 (August 2008): 466–475. doi: 10.1038/ncponc1134.

34. Childre, Doc. *De-Stress Kit for the Changing Times.* Institute of HeartMath, 2008: 13. Accessed January 15, 2015. nwmedicalhypnosis.com/documents/destress-kit.pdf.

35. Villeneuve, Paul, David A. Agnew, Anthony B. Miller, Paul N. Corey, and James T. Purdham. "Leukemia in electric utility workers: The evaluation of alternative indices of exposure to 60 Hz electric and magnetic fields." *American Journal of Industrial Medicine* 37, no. 6 (June 2000): 607–617. doi: 10.1002/(SICI)1097-0274(200006)37:6<607::AID-AJIM5>3.0.CO;2-L.

36. Villeneuve, Paul, David A. Agnew, Anthony B. Miller, and Paul N. Corey. N. "Non-Hodgkin's Lymphoma Among Electric Utility Workers in Ontario: the Evaluation of Alternate Indices of Exposure to 60 Hz Electric and Magnetic Fields." *Occupational and Environmental Medicine* 57, no.4 (April 2000): 249–257. doi:10.1136/oem.57.4.249.

37. Maté, Gabor. *When the Body Says No: Exploring the Stress-Disease Connection.* Hoboken: John Wiley & Sons, Inc., 2003: 38.

38. "Youth Violence and Alcohol Fact Sheet." World Health Organization. 2006:1. Accessed January 16, 2015. who.int/violence_injury_prevention/violence/world_report/factsheets/ft_youth.pdf.

39. "Youth Risk Behavior Surveillance—2013." Centers for Disease Control and Prevention. *Morbidity and Mortality Weekly Report Surveillance Summaries*, 63, no. 4:11–12. Accessed January 15, 2015. cdc.gov/mmwr/pdf/ss/ss6304.pdf.

40. "Leading Causes of Death Reports, National and Regional, 1999–2012." Centers for Disease Control and Prevention. Accessed January 15, 2015. webappa.cdc.gov/sasweb/ncipc/leadcaus10_us.html.

41. Bridgeland, John M., John J. Dilulio, and Karen Burke Morison. "The Silent Epidemic: Perspectives of High School Dropouts." Washington, D.C.: Civic Enterprises, LLC, March 2006: iii. Accessed January 15, 2015. docs.gatesfoundation.org/Documents/thesilentepidemic3-06final.pdf.

42. Hawkins, J. David, John W. Graham, Eugene Maguin, Robert Abbott, Karl G. Hill, and Richard F. Catalano. "Exploring the effects of age of alcohol use initiation and psychosocial risk factors on subsequent alcohol misuse." *Journal of Studies on Alcohol* 58, no. 3 (1997):280–290.

43. "Advanced Social and Emotional Learning: Strategic Approach." NoVo Foundation. January 2012. Accessed January 13, 2015. novofoundation.org/advancing-social-and-emotional-learning/strategic-approach.

44. Stern, Robin. "Social and Emotional Learning: What is it? How can we use it to help our children?" NYU Child Study Center. Accessed January 15, 2015. aboutourkids.org/articles/social_emotional_learning_what_it_how_can_we_use_it_help_our_children.

45. Bridgeland, John, Mary Bruce, and Arya Hariharan. "The Missing Piece: A National Teacher Survey on How Social and Emotional Learning Can Empower Children and Transform Schools: A Report for CASEL." Chicago: Civic Enterprises, 2013:5. Accessed January 15, 2015. http://static1.squarespace.com/static/513f79f9e4b05ce7b70e9673/t/526a2589e4b01768fee91a6a/1382688137983/the-missing-piece.pdf.

46. "BePeace (The Connection Practice) at Oakley Elementary School." YouTube Video, 5:23. Posted by Rasur Foundation International, December 30, 2014. youtu.be/0rs-o-f4TZg.

47. "Workplace Conflict and How Businesses Can Harness It to Thrive." Consulting Psychologists Press, July 2008:3. Accessed January 15, 2015. cpp.com/pdfs/CPP_Global_Human_Capital_Report_Workplace_Conflict.pdf.

48. Anders, George. "The Number One Job Skill in 2020." LinkedIn, June 11, 2013. Accessed January 16, 2015. linkedin.com/today/post/article/20130611180041-59549-the-no-1-job-skill-in-2020?trk=tod-home-art-large_0.

49. Culture of Empathy Builder: Daniel Goleman. Culture of Empathy. November 26, 2014. Accessed January 16, 2015. http://cultureofempathy.com/references/Experts/Daniel-Goleman.htm.

50. Goleman, 2006: xii.

51. Baer, Drake. "Emotional Intelligence Predicts Job Success: Do You Have It?" Fast Company, December 16, 2013. Accessed January 16, 2015. fastcompany.com/3023335/leadership-now/emotional-intelligence-predicts-job-success-do-you-have-it.

52. Kriegel, Robert J., and David Brandt. *Sacred Cows Make the Best Burgers: Developing Change-Ready People and Organizations.* (Google eBook). Grand Central Publishing, 2008. Accessed January 16, 2015. http://books.google.com/books?id=0mU1M1aQw7kC&printsec=frontcover&source=gbs_ge_summary_r&cad=0#v=onepage&q&f=false.

53. Crabb, Larry. *Connecting: Healing for Ourselves and Our Relationships, a Radical New Vision*. Nashville: W Publishing Group, 1997. Kindle edition. Locations 3686–3687, 186–187, and 3792–3793.

54. Bohm, David, "Interviews: Touch the Future." Accessed January 15, 2015, ttfuture.org/authors/david_bohm. Adapted from an informal talk given by professor Bohm in Santa Monica, California in 1981. Also included are several brief passages from two additional sources: Thought as A System (1990), and Changing Consciousness (1991).

55. Brenes Mesén, 1998.

56. UNICEF. 2015. "Communication for Development." UNICEF Bosnia and Herzegovina—Resources. Accessed February 18, 2015. http://www.unicef.org/bih/resources_24836.html.

57. "Resolution Adopted by the General Assembly: 52/13. Culture of Peace." United Nations, 1998. Accessed January 15, 2015. http://www3.unesco.org/iycp/kits/res52-13_en.htm.

58. Sherman, Lawrence W., and Heather Strang. "Restorative Justice: The Evidence." London: The Smith Institute. 2007; p. 63. Accessed January 16, 2015. iirp.edu/pdf/RJ_full_report.pdf.

59. "Delivers First Civic Center for Peace in Garabito." Ministry of Justice and Peace, Republic of Costa Rica. April 29, 2014. Accessed January 16, 2015. mjp.go.cr/Informacion/VisorNoticias.aspx?new=38.

60. "Workshop Training of Trainers in Community Mediation and Multi-Party Mediation." Ministry of Justice and Peace, Republic of Costa Rica. October 31, 2014. Accessed January 16, 2015. mjpmjp.go.cr/Informacion/VisorNoticias.aspx?new=132.

61. Camus, Albert, *The Myth of Sisyphus and Other Essays*. Translated by Justin O'Brien. New York: Vintage Books, 1991:202.

Glossary

Coherence: A state when the heart, mind and emotions are in focused alignment and cooperation; they are synchronized.

Empathy: The ability to feel into your own, or another person's experience, without identifying with it.

Heart-Brain Insight: A process that begins with heart-brain coherence, moves into asking, "What do I need to know?" and inner listening, and then receiving an idea that can be applied in your life.

Integrated Honesty: Honesty that takes into account the needs of both people involved in a conflict, as well as any new insights about the issue.

Rasur: A person who is certified by Rasur Foundation International to be a coach, trainer and/or curriculum instructor of the Connection Practice and BePeace. This name comes from "Rasur," a Costa Rican poem about a mythical teacher who was skilled at the art of connection.

Restorative Justice: A conflict-resolution process that builds relationship between the parties in conflict and, if possible, restores what was damaged or harmed.

Self-Empathy: The process of naming and experiencing our own feelings and needs.

Social-Emotional Intelligence: How well we handle ourselves—our feelings and needs—and how well we interact with others.

Social and Emotional Learning (SEL): Education that builds social and emotional intelligence so that we can effectively manage our inner lives, see the impact of our choices, enrich our relationships, and maintain a positive outlook.

Stand-Up Honesty: Speaking up that combines courage, empathy for the other person, and judgment-free honesty.

The BePeace Practice: The version of the Connection Practice that is taught in spiritual settings. BePeace doesn't promote a specific belief but acknowledges that personal growth can be linked to spiritual growth.

The Connection Practice: A scientifically based method that combines empathy and insight to build social and emotional intelligence.

The Connection Practice is made up of three activities:

1. The Connection Process—the steps for uniting empathy and insight to resolve daily challenges and celebrate life.

2. The Connection Path—a tool for resolving difficult conflicts with others, or within yourself, through a progressive experience of empathy and insight.

3. The Connection Mediation—conflict intervention that integrates empathy and insight.

Book Study

As this book study advances from week to week, and the participants become more skilled at the Connection Practice, the content below becomes more experiential. Consequently, the early chapters have an abundance of discussion questions, while the later chapters have fewer questions and more activities.

Chapter 1: From Confusion to Connection

1. How do you define connection?

2. What lack of connection have you experienced in your past? In your present? What are the consequences you have faced from lack of connection in those situations?

3. What lack of connection do you see in your community? Your country? The world? What are the consequences you have observed from these situations?

4. What methods have you used to stay connected to yourself? To others?

5. Have you ever been bullied or known someone who was? Have you ever bullied someone? What were the outcomes of these interactions? Were you satisfied with them? If not, how could they have been different?

6. Have you ever felt like you wasted your life because you were stuck in a problem for too long? What happened? What would have helped?

7. What outcomes might result from learning to connect to yourself and others?

Chapter 2: Heart-Brain Coherence Leads to Insight

1. Are you aware of painful memories that you sometimes re-experience in the present? When you are triggered by something that reminds you of the past, do you act irrationally? How would you like to respond instead? Can you imagine being free of that reaction?

2. Think of a problem in your life and write down the best solution you know for it.

3. Choose something that is easy for you to appreciate, something that elicits a warm feeling. Then try the three steps of the Quick Coherence technique, taking plenty of time for each step: Heart Focus, Heart Breathing, Heart Feeling (further details on page 79). How did that feel?

4. Return to the problem that you wrote down in number 2. Access an insight by beginning with the steps of Quick Coherence. When you believe you are coherent, ask your heart what you need to know about that problem. Listen and, when your answer comes, write it down. Does this answer differ from the one in number 2? In what way?

5. How do insights come to you? In a picture? In words? With a strong feeling?

6. Do you wonder sometimes whether you have accessed an insight or whether you just made something up with your mind? Think about a time when you had an insight that you were confident was true and powerful. How did you feel after it came to you? Now consider a time when you thought of a solution, but there was no special feeling afterwards. Does this help you to discern the difference between the two experiences?

7. Have you ever had an "aha" that changed your life? What were you feeling just prior to having the insight?

8. Have you ever received an insight through a dream? If so, please describe it. What do you think stimulated you to have this dream?

9. Have you ever acted on an insight and it didn't turn out as you had hoped? What happened? What would you do differently next time?

10. Have you ever had an insight that you only understood with hindsight?

Chapter 3: Naming Feelings and Needs Leads to Empathy

1. What is the most memorable experience you've had of receiving empathy from someone? How did it differ from how other people responded to you?

2. Think of a recent situation that is still alive with negative feelings. Using the lists provided on pages 48, 49 and 50, write down all your feelings and all your needs here. Then notice how you feel afterwards. If you have less of a negative charge about the circumstances, you have just experienced self-empathy in meeting a challenge.

3. Do step 2 again but use a situation that has positive feelings. How do you feel afterwards?

4. How do you feel when you name a need? Do you find yourself meeting your needs in unconscious ways, such as addictions to food, alcohol, drugs and cigarettes?

5. Choose a partner who will play a person that you are in conflict with. Explain the conflict. Then try respectfully guessing the feelings and needs of the person who

is troubling you, using the feelings and needs lists. Ask your partner for feedback on whether your empathy was effective.

6. Have you ever experienced getting stuck in negative feelings? How did you find your way out?

7. What is your most frequent habitual response to other people's problems? Advice? Minimizing the situation? Educating them? Sharing a similar problem that you've had? How do you feel when others respond in that way to your problems?

8. Can you think of a time that you blamed someone else for not meeting your needs? What other options were available to you for meeting those needs?

9. Have you ever stuffed your honesty? Have you ever expressed your honesty as an attack on someone? Think of someone you would like to express your honesty to, but you're hesitant to do it. Use the Quick Coherence technique and ask what you need to know about that. Listen and then write down your answer. What did you find out?

10. Have you tried giving empathy first in a conflict and then your honesty? How did it go? What's easier for you: giving empathy or expressing honesty? Why?

Chapter 4: Empathy + Insight = Connection

1. Which inner strength have you tended to rely on most in your life, empathy or insight? Can you remember a time when you needed the balance of the other strength?

2. Have you experienced situations where you were so upset that you didn't want to calm down? What was the result?

3. Have you had an experience where you or another person expressed intuition in an arrogant way? What happened?

4. Have you had experiences or witnessed another person's experience where empathy seemed to turn into misery? What happened?

5. Think of a moment in your life when you were at your very best. Then do the first two steps of the Quick Coherence technique. When you get to the third step, use the object of your appreciation that you normally use. Then, once you have achieved coherence, begin appreciating that moment you were shining as a human being. Stay in that state of self-appreciation as long as you can. Afterwards, share this experience with a supportive person.

6. Can you remember a time when you got attached to a particular strategy for getting a need met or resolving an issue? What happened?

7. Is there a need that you often experience as unmet, such as emotional safety, acceptance, respect, trust or support? Can you remember a trauma in your life that created the perception that this need would not be met? What strategy could you use to teach yourself that this need can be met?

8. What are the outcomes when we live from an "all about me" perspective? An "all about you" perspective? An "all about us" perspective? What are the benefits and drawbacks of these perspectives?

9. Do you feel a need for change in your life? If so, do you see the Connection Practice as a helpful tool for navigating those changes?

Chapter 5: Using the Connection Practice to Overcome Challenges

1. Have you ever had a painful betrayal? Use the Connection Process outline on page 214. How do you feel now?

2. Have you ever attempted to heal a physical illness through inner work? How did you go about it? Was it successful? Would the Connection Practice have helped you heal?

3. Do you have a challenge right now that you would like to address with the Connection Process? Find a partner and use the worksheet on the next page to help you process this challenge.

4. Do you have difficulty taking daily time to reflect on your personal growth? Why or why not? Do you have a special place to sit where you reflect on life? If not, is there a place in your home where you could create one? Are you interested in using the Connection Process as a daily practice? Why or why not?

5. Does it help you to talk out loud when you process? Do you have a picture or some other object that you talk to that helps you focus?

6. When you are overwhelmed with emotions, what physical activity helps you cope? Are you able to address your emotions during or after that activity?

7. Would you like to practice connection with a partner? Do you have a partner that you can practice with? If not, can you think of someone who could serve in that capacity?

8. Do you know of a Connection Practice group in your area? If so, would you consider joining the group for

The Connection Process with a Partner

Person Who Shares	Partner
1. Concisely share your challenge or celebration with your partner. Avoid getting into story because each sharer will need about 15 minutes for the process.	Listen with an open heart. Be present. Guess feelings and needs by asking, "Are you feeling . . . because you need . . . ?"
2. Respond to guesses honestly.	
3. If another person is involved in the issue, guess his/her feelings and needs.	Help guess the feelings and needs of the other person in the issue.
4. Partner leads Quick Coherence technique to help sharer achieve heart coherence: "Focus on your heart, breathe through your heart and feel appreciation."	
5. Access Heart-Brain Insight by asking, "What do I need to know?" Listen for the answer. Share your insight with your partner.	Remain in coherence.
6.	Ask if the insight met your partner's needs. If there are still unmet needs or the person wants more clarity, do a Heart-Brain Insight again.
7. Share your plan to act on the answer. If the issue involves another person and you plan to talk to that person, remember to give empathy first and honesty second.	Support your partner as appropriate.

regular practice? If not, would you consider starting one if you had a Rasur to lead the group?

9. What do you have to celebrate today? Using the lists in chapter 3, identify your feelings and your met needs, get coherent, and listen for an insight. Did you get more juice from this happy moment in your life?

10. Think of a time when you asked yourself, "What's wrong with me?" in regard to any issue in your life. Now ask, "What was going on with me?" How is your response different?

Chapter 6: Creating Connection at School and at Home

1. What solutions do you think would work best to reduce violence in schools?

2. Do you still have painful memories from your school days? Find a partner and ask him or her to role-play whoever it was that hurt you. The partner's job is to hear you explain what happened and then guess your feelings and needs about it, using the feelings and needs lists in chapter 3.

3. Do you have a vision of an ideal school? Would it include social-emotional learning? How do you see this vision unfolding?

4. Do you still have painful memories from the parenting you received? Find a partner and ask him or her to role-play one of your parents. The partner's job is to hear you explain what happened and then guess your feelings and needs, using the lists from chapter three. Now try guessing the feelings and needs of your parent. After achieving empathy for yourself and your parent, move into

coherence and listen for an insight. Share your insight with your partner. How do you see it now?

Chapter 7: Connection in Business, Nonprofits, Government and Higher Education

1. Have you had a conflict in business that didn't go well? Find a partner who will play the person you are in conflict with in a role-play. Describe the situation to your partner. Then, using the feelings and needs lists, guess the feelings and needs of the person you are in conflict with. After your empathy hits home with your partner, express your honesty by saying what happened, how you felt and what you need or value. Use the lists to help you stay focused on feelings and needs and not wander into judgments and blame. Remember that in expressing your honesty, you need to choose words that will build on the connection rather than create division. At the end of the role-play, assess whether you were able to build a stronger connection.

2. Do you know of businesses that have conflict resolution policies? How would those policies change if the Connection Practice were integrated into the organization?

3. What benefits do you see for groups using Heart-Brain Insight in business? What strategies would you use to introduce this approach to business people?

4. After reading this chapter, how well do you think the Connection Practice would fit in the cultures of business, government, nonprofits and higher education?

5. Imagine that you have an appointment to speak to a politician about the Connection Practice. Find a

partner to play the politician with you at this meeting. The partner's job is to hear you explain your view about violence in schools and the need for social and emotional learning as a solution. Then your partner will guess your feelings and needs about it, using the lists from chapter three. Now try guessing the feelings and needs of the politician. Afterwards, move into coherence and listen for an insight. Share your insight with your partner.

Chapter 8: The BePeace Practice

1. Have you ever had a conflict within your spiritual community that didn't go well? How could the BePeace Practice have made a difference?

2. Do you have any painful memories of experiences in a faith-based community? Find a partner and ask him or her to role-play whoever it was that hurt you. The partner's job is to hear you explain what happened and then guess your feelings and needs about it, using the feelings and needs lists in chapter three. After the empathy lands, move into coherence together and listen for an insight. Share your insight with your partner. How do you see it now?

3. Have you ever had an insight that seemed to be spiritual in nature?

4. How would you like to see the BePeace Practice used in your spiritual community?

5. How could the BePeace Practice be used to heal conflicts between religions?

Chapter 9: Toward a More Connected World

1. What would a more connected world look like to you?

2. Do you agree with the quote from David Bohm? Why or why not?

3. How would you use the Connection Practice for social change? Do you agree with the concept of restorative justice?

4. What would it take to focus the media on connection?

5. In the "Inside out, bottom up, top down and all around" model described in pages 198–204, where do you see yourself?

6. Imagine that you will be speaking with the leader of your country about the Connection Practice. Find a partner to role-play this conversation. Begin by asking the leader about his or her greatest concerns. After that, your job is to listen and to guess the feelings and needs of the leader, using the lists from chapter three. Once the needs have been confirmed, you will share how you think the Connection Practice could help. When you are finished, ask your partner for feedback on how it went.

Chapter 10: A New Beginning

1. Is there any aspect of your life that has felt comfortless? What breakthroughs have you had in your ability to embody connection? What are you still yearning to model in your life?

2. Are you experiencing any resistance to looking inside? If so, move into coherence and ask yourself what you need to know about that. What did you discover?

3. Are you considering becoming a certified Connection Practice Coach, Trainer or Curriculum Instructor? Where would you want to offer the Connection Practice? What is your next step?

4. Do you have any concerns about using the Connection Practice in your life or teaching it? Find a partner and do the Connection Process with a Partner (see steps on page 235 to process that question).

5. Express one thing that you appreciate about each person in your book study group. Create a closing activity, such as singing a song or sharing a meal, that expresses the connection you've experienced together.

Resources

The Connection Practice, Compassion, and Empathy

Armstrong, Karen. *Twelve Steps to a Compassionate Life*. 2010.

Arpa, Maria. *The Heart of Mindful Relationships: Meditations on Togetherness*. 2012.

Barasch, Marc. *Field Notes on the Compassionate Life: A Search for the Soul of Kindness*. 2005.

Brown, Brené. *Daring Greatly: How the Courage to Be Vulnerable Transforms the Way We Live, Love, Parent, and Lead*. 2012.

Brown, Brené. *The Gifts of Imperfection: Let Go of Who You Think You're Supposed to Be and Embrace Who You Are*. 2010.

Bryson, Kelly. *Don't Be Nice, Be Real: Balancing Passion for Self with Passion for Others*. 2002.

Connor, Jane Marantz and Killian Dian. *Connecting Across Differences: Finding Common Ground with Anyone, Anywhere, Anytime*. 2012.

De Waal, Frans. *The Age of Empathy: Nature's Lessons for a Kinder Society*. 2009.

Decety, Jean (editor). *Empathy*. 2011.

Decety, Jean and Ickes, William (editors). *The Social Neuroscience of Empathy*. 2011.

Eckert, Holly Michelle. *Graduating from Guilt: Six Steps to Overcome Guilt and Reclaim Your Life*. 2010.

Engler, Carol. *The First Turning: A Vision of America and the World at Peace*. 2014.

Dalton, Jane & Fairchild, Lyn. *The Compassionate Classroom: Lessons That Nurture Wisdom and Empathy*. 2004.

Gilbert, Paul. *The Compassionate Mind (Compassion-Focused Therapy)*. 2009.

Goleman, Daniel. *Emotional Intelligence: 10th Anniversary Edition*. 2005.

Gordon, Mary. *Roots of Empathy: Changing the World Child by Child*. 2012.

Iacoboni, Marco. *Mirroring People: The Science of Empathy and How We Connect with Others*. 2009.

Johnson, Rita Marie. *The Return of Rasur* (also *El Regreso de Rasur*). 2000.

Keysers, Christian. *The Empathic Brain*. 2011.

Krznaric, Roman. *Empathy: Why It Matters, and How to Get It*. 2014.

McLaren, Karen. *The Art of Empathy: A Complete Guide to Life's Most Essential Skill*. 2013.

Miyashiro, Marie. *The Empathy Factor: Your Competitive Advantage for Personal, Team, and Business Success*. 2011.

Patnaik, Dev. *Wired to Care: How Companies Prosper When They Create Widespread Empathy*. 2009.

Perry, Bruce and Szalavitz, Maia. *Born for Love*. 2010.

Rifkin, Jeremy. *The Empathic Civilization: The Race to Global Consciousness in a World in Crisis*. 2009.

Nonviolent Communication

D'Ansembourg, Thomas. *Being Genuine: Stop Being Nice, Start Being Real*. 2007.

Goodfriend, Rick. *I Hear You, But: Nonviolent Communication and Listening Skills: Tips for Improving All Relationships*. 2009.

Hart, Sura and Victoria Kindle Hodson. *The Compassionate Classroom: Relationship Based Teaching and Learning*. 2004.

Hart, Sura, and Victoria Kindle Hodson. *Respectful Parents, Respectful Kids*. 2006.

Hart, Sura, and Victoria Kindle Hodson. *The No-Fault Classroom: Tools to Resolve Conflict and Foster Relationship Intelligence*. 2008.

Kashtan, Inbal. *Parenting from Your Heart: Sharing the Gifts of Compassion, Connection, and Choice*. 2003.

Kashtan, Miki. *Spinning Threads of Radical Aliveness: Transcending the Legacy of Separation in Our Individual Lives*. 2014.

Klein, Shari, and Neill Gibson. *What's Making You Angry? Ten Steps to Transforming Anger So Everyone Wins.* 2003.

Larsson, Liv. *A Helping Hand: Mediation with Nonviolent Communication.* 2010.

Lasater, Ike K., and Judith Hanson Lasater. *What We Say Matters: Practicing Nonviolent Communication.* 2009.

Lasater, Ike. *Words That Work in Business: A Practical Guide to Effective Communication in the Workplace.* 2010

Leu, Lucy. *Nonviolent Communication Companion Workbook.* 2003.

Mackenzie, Mary. *Peaceful Living: Daily Meditations for Living with Love, Healing, and Compassion.* 2005.

Prieto, Jaime L. *The Joy of Compassionate Connecting: The Way of Christ Through Nonviolent Communication.* 2010.

Rosenberg, Marshall. *Being Me, Loving You: A Practical Guide to Extraordinary Relationships.* 2005.

Rosenberg, Marshall. *Getting Past the Pain Between Us: Healing and Reconciliation Without Compromise.* 2003.

Rosenberg, Marshall. *The Heart of Social Change: How to Make a Difference in Your World.* 2003.

Rosenberg, Marshall. *Life-Enriching Education: Nonviolent Communication Helps Schools Improve Performance, Reduce Conflict, and Enhance Relationships.* 2003.

Rosenberg, Marshall. *Nonviolent Communication: A Language of Life.* 2003.

Rosenberg, Marshall. *Speak Peace in a World of Conflict.* 2005.

Rosenberg, Marshall. *The Surprising Purpose of Anger: Beyond Anger Management: Finding the Gift.* 2005.

Rosenberg, Marshall. *We Can Work It Out: Resolving Conflicts Peacefully and Powerfully.* 2003.

Sears, Mel. *Humanizing Health Care: Creating Cultures of Compassion with Nonviolent Communication.* 2010.

van Deusen Hunsinger, Deborah, and Theresa F. Latini. *Transforming Church Conflict: Compassionate Leadership in Action.* 2013.

HeartMath and Heart Intelligence

Childre, Doc and Martin, Beech. *The HeartMath Solution.* 1999.

Childre, Doc. *Teaching Children to Love: 80 Games & Fun Activities for Raising Balanced Children in Unbalanced Times.* 1996.

Childre, Doc and Rozman, Deborah. *Transforming Anxiety: The HeartMath Solution for Overcoming Fear and Worry and Creating Serenity.* 2006.

Childre, Doc and Rozman, Deborah. *Transforming Depression: The HeartMath Solution to Feeling Overwhelmed, Sad, and Stressed.* 2007.

Childre (née Paddison), Sara. *The Hidden Power of the Heart.* 1998. Also e-book.

McCraty, Rollin. *The Coherent Heart: Heart-Brain Interactions, Psychophysiological Coherence, and the Emergence of System-Wide Order.* 2012.

Pearce, Joseph C. *The Biology of Transcendence: A Blueprint of the Human Spirit.* 2004.

Pearce, Joseph C. *The Heart-Mind Matrix: How the Heart Can Teach the Mind New Ways to Think.* 2012.

Pearsall, Paul. *The Heart's Code: Tapping the Wisdom and Power of Our Heart Energy.* 1999.

Suggested Websites

For the most current links, see
rasurinternational.org/suggested-websites.

Websites for the Connection Practice, Compassion, and Empathy

Center for Compassion and Altruism Research and Education (Stanford): ccare.stanford.edu/#1

Culture of Empathy, many resources here on empathy; website from Edwin Rutsch: cultureofempathy.com

Empathy as a Factor for Change, research on empathy and

compassion: slideshare.net/LidewijNiezink/london
-l-niezink-2012-empathy-as-a-factor-for-change-slideshare
Empathy Library, books and films regarding empathy:
empathylibrary.com
Greater Good: Research about empathy and compassion,
among other things: greatergood.berkeley.edu/about
Rasur Foundation International: rasurinternational.org

Websites for Nonviolent Communication

Bay NVC (training organization in the Bay Area of California):
baynvc.org
Center for Nonviolent Communication website: cnvc.org
Jim Manske and Jori Manske's website, NVC trainers; many
resources for listening and reading: radicalcompassion.com.
Based in Hawaii.
Maine NVC Network; resources and articles available:
mainenvcnetwork.org/index.htm
NVC Academy—a wealth of online resources and tele-classes
from Certified NVC trainers: nvctraining.com
NVC Boston, a group of NVC trainers who offer workshops
and classes in Massachusetts and New York: nvc.boston.org
NVC Dance Floors, info on the NVC Dance Floors, developed
by Bridget Belgrave and Gina Lawrie (kinesthetic way to
learn NVC): nvcdancefloors.com
Restorative Circles (which are inspired by the principles of
NVC and the principles of restorative justice) and Dominic
Barter: restorativecircles.org
Robert Gonzalez's website, based in Portland, Oregon, offers
training related to embodied spirituality at the root of NVC:
living-compassion.org.
Speaking Peace, NVC organization in Ohio which offers many
trainings: speakingpeace.org
Sura Hart and Victoria Kindle Hodson's website:
thenofaultzone.com

Websites for HeartMath and Heart Intelligence

The Institute of HeartMath in Belgium, the Netherlands, Germany and Luxembourg: heartmathbenelux.com.

The Institute of HeartMath in Mexico: corente.mx

The Institute of HeartMath research: heartmath.org

The Institute of HeartMath products and services: heartmath.com

About the Author

Rita Marie Johnson is all about making connections. As an educator, author, speaker, award-winning innovator, and founder and CEO of Rasur Foundation International, she creates and shares powerful, practical solutions for key personal and societal challenges. She has been sharing her ideas and methods worldwide for more than ten years.

What began as an effort to research more peaceful solutions to human conflict has evolved into a remarkable method for connecting our enormous intelligence with our equally enormous capacity for empathy. In short, when we connect with ourselves, we increase our ability and willingness to connect with others.

She discovered that the resulting synergy of connecting mind and heart, feelings and needs, and insight and empathy maximizes our social-emotional intelligence, builds resilience and enhances performance. Called the Connection Practice®, her method is now being used by individuals, schools, businesses, and organizations to enhance personal well-being, reduce conflicts and bullying, improve communication and collaboration, and boost performance.

In 2004, Johnson began offering this methodology in Costa Rican public schools. Now close to 1,500 teachers have been trained, impacting nearly 40,000 students. Annual evaluations revealed that bullying, intolerance, conflicts, violence and misconduct reports had decreased.

The Connection Practice earned the Ashoka Changemakers Innovation Award, chosen from 79 projects in 32 countries.

Johnson initiated a bill in 2006 to establish a Ministry for Peace in Costa Rica, which was embraced by President Oscar Arias, Nobel Peace Prize laureate. The bill passed in 2009.

In 2010, Johnson began teaching the Connection Practice Foundations Course at the UN-mandated University for Peace in Costa Rica, a graduate school for international leaders.

Through trainers certified by RFI, the Connection Practice is spreading rapidly in the United States. In 2012, the first school pilot project in Houston was deemed a success. St. Rita School in Fort Worth was the next to adopt the practice, and now schools in Florida, California, Wisconsin, and other states are implementing the curriculum. The Connection Practice has also been adopted in addiction recovery centers, nonprofits working on domestic violence, faith-based communities, therapeutic massage institutes and after-school programs.

In addition to presenting seminars in the U.S.A., Canada, Central America, Europe, and Japan, Johnson was a keynote speaker at the Department of Peace Conference in Washington DC, the Global Summit for Ministries and Departments for Peace in 2009 and a Rotary International conference in 2013. Audiences everywhere have embraced her authenticity and unique solutions.

Completely Connected: Uniting Our Empathy and Insight for Extraordinary Results tells her story and lays out the key features and benefits of the Connection Practice. Johnson lives in Costa Rica and works globally, with headquarters for Rasur Foundation International in Dallas, Texas.

To learn more, visit rasurinternational.org.

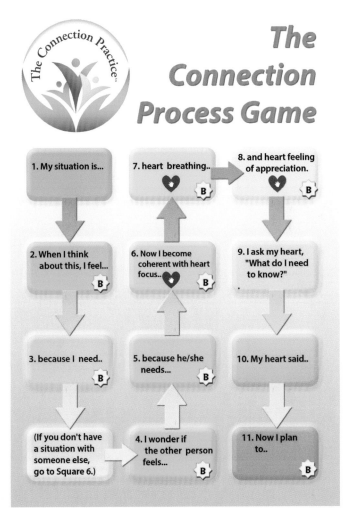

The Connection Practice™

The Connection Process Game

1. My situation is...

2. When I think about this, I feel... **B**

3. because I need.. **B**

(If you don't have a situation with someone else, go to Square 6.)

4. I wonder if the other person feels... **B**

5. because he/she needs... **B**

6. Now I become coherent with heart focus.. **B**

7. heart breathing.. **B**

8. and heart feeling of appreciation. **B**

9. I ask my heart, "What do I need to know?"

10. My heart said..

11. Now I plan to.. **B**

When students play this game each morning,
they feel heard and know they matter.
(See explanation in text on page 131.)
Copyright © 2015 Rasur Foundation International

The Vision of Rasur Foundation International:

A world where each person practices the art of connection and passes this gift on to the next generation

Costa Rican students Douglas and Brenda model connection.

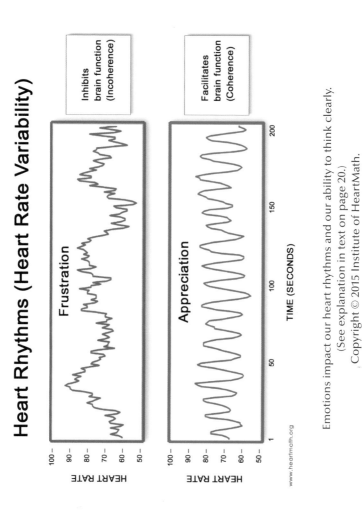

Heart Rhythms (Heart Rate Variability)

Frustration

Inhibits
brain function
(Incoherence)

Appreciation

Facilitates
brain function
(Coherence)

TIME (SECONDS)

HEART RATE

HEART RATE

www.heartmath.org

Emotions impact our heart rhythms and our ability to think clearly.
(See explanation in text on page 20.)
Copyright © 2015 Institute of HeartMath.

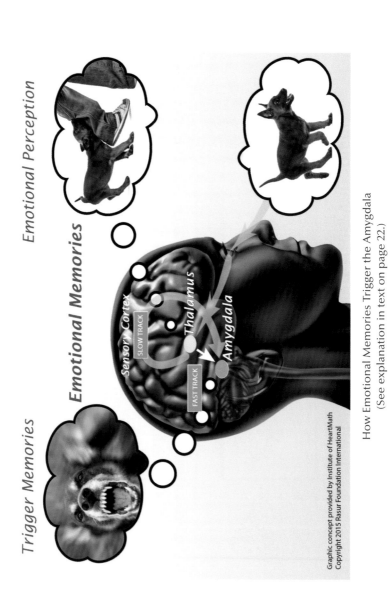

How Emotional Memories Trigger the Amygdala
(See explanation in text on page 22.)

Graphic concept provided by Institute of HeartMath
Copyright 2015 Rasur Foundation International

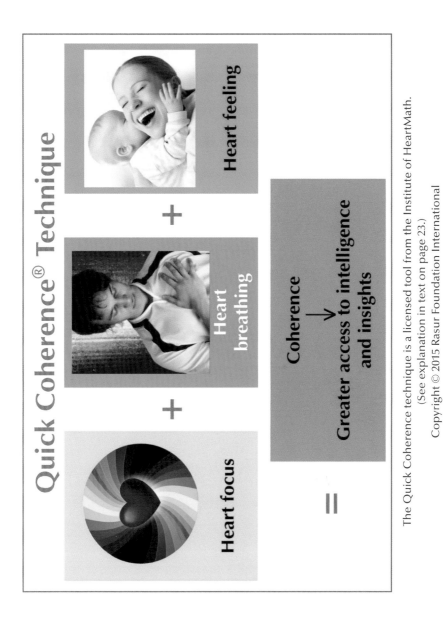

Quick Coherence® Technique

Heart focus + Heart breathing + Heart feeling

Coherence → Greater access to intelligence and insights =

The Quick Coherence technique is a licensed tool from the Institute of HeartMath.
(See explanation in text on page 23.)
Copyright © 2015 Rasur Foundation International

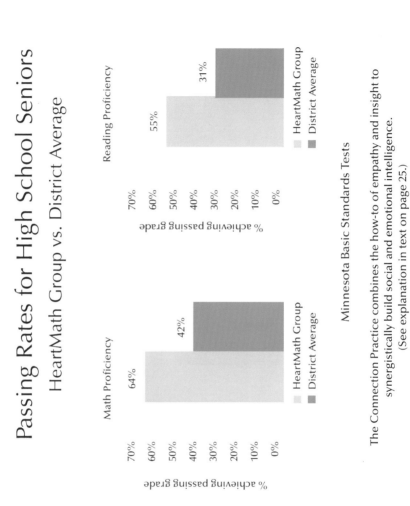

Passing Rates for High School Seniors
HeartMath Group vs. District Average

Math Proficiency

% achieving passing grade

- 70%
- 60%
- 50%
- 40%
- 30%
- 20%
- 10%
- 0%

64%
42%

■ HeartMath Group
■ District Average

Reading Proficiency

% achieving passing grade

- 70%
- 60%
- 50%
- 40%
- 30%
- 20%
- 10%
- 0%

55%
31%

■ HeartMath Group
■ District Average

Minnesota Basic Standards Tests

The Connection Practice combines the how-to of empathy and insight to synergistically build social and emotional intelligence.
(See explanation in text on page 25.)

Completely Connected

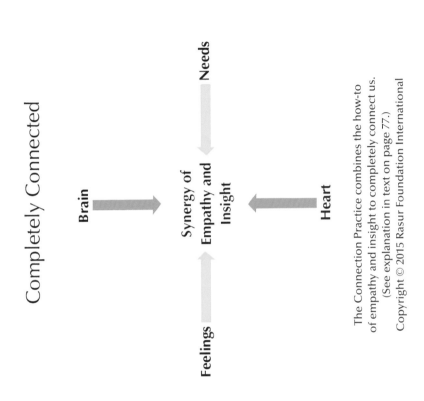

Brain → **Synergy of Empathy and Insight** ← **Heart**

Feelings → **Synergy of Empathy and Insight** ← **Needs**

The Connection Practice combines the how-to of empathy and insight to completely connect us. (See explanation in text on page 77.)

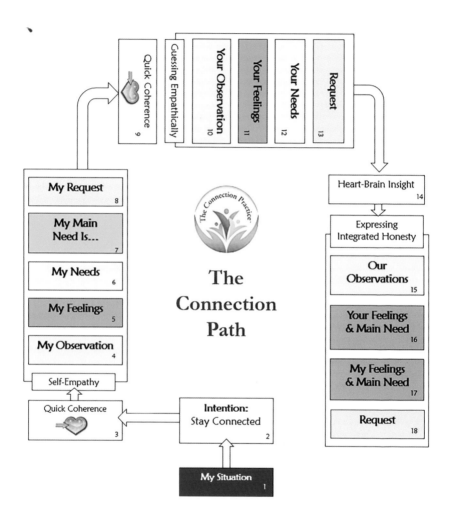

The Connection Path is used for conflict resolution,
whether it is an inner conflict or conflict with another person.
(See explanation in text on page 81.)
Copyright © 2015 Rasur Foundation International